CATHOLIC
SUNDAY MASS READINGS
FOR 2025

CW01550031

(SUNDAY MISSAL 2024 – 2025)

**Catholic Sunday Mass Readings for 2025
with the Principal Celebrations of the Liturgical Year C,
in 2025**

Compiled by

Catholic Lectionary Publishers

CONTENTS

Section A

Section B

PRINCIPAL CELEBRATIONS OF THE LITURGICAL YEAR C, 2025

CELEBRATIONS	DATE
First Sunday of Advent, Year C	December 1, 2024
Ash Wednesday	March 5, 2025
Easter Sunday	April 20, 2025
The Ascension of the Lord	June 1, 2025
Pentecost Sunday	June 8, 2025
The Most Holy Body and Blood of Christ (*Corpus Christi*)	June 22, 2025
First Sunday of Advent, Year A	November 30, 2025

SUNDAY MASS READINGS FOR 2024 - 2025
First Sunday of Advent, Year C

First Reading: Jeremiah 33:14-16

[14] The days are coming, says the LORD,
    when I will fulfill the promise
    I made to the house of Israel and Judah.
[15] In those days, at that time,
    I will raise up for David a just shoot;
    he shall do what is right and just in the
        land.
[16] In those days Judah shall be safe
    and Jerusalem shall dwell secure;
    this is the name they shall call her:
    "The LORD our justice."

Responsorial Psalm: Psalms 25:4-5, 8-9, 10, 14

R. [1b] To you, O Lord, I lift my soul.

[4] Yours ways, O LORD, make known to me;
    teach me your paths.
[5] guide me in your truth and teach me,
    for you are God my savior,
    and for you I wait all the day.

R. To you, O Lord, I lift my soul.

[8] Good and upright is the LORD,
    thus he shows sinners the way,
[9] He guides the humble in justice,
    and teaches the humble his way.

R. To you, O Lord, I lift my soul.

[10] All the paths of the Lord are kindness and
        constancy
    toward those who keep his covenant and
        his decrees.
[14] The friendship of the LORD is with those who
        fear him;
    and his covenant, for their instruction.

R. To you, O Lord, I lift my soul.

Second Reading: 1 Thessalonians 3:12-4:2

Brothers and sisters, [12] May the Lord make you increase and abound in love for one another and for all, just as we have for you, [13] so as to strengthen your hearts, to be blameless in holiness before our God and Father at the coming of our Lord Jesus with all his holy ones. Amen.

[1] Finally, brothers and sisters, we earnestly ask and exhort you in the Lord Jesus that, as you received from us how you should conduct yourselves to please God—and as you are conducting yourselves—you do so even more. [2] For you know what instructions we gave you through the Lord Jesus.

Alleluia: Psalms 85:8

R. Alleluia, alleluia.
[8] Show us, Lord, your love;
and grant us your salvation.
R. Alleluia, alleluia.

Gospel: Luke 21:25-28, 34-36

Jesus said to his disciples: [25] "There will be signs in the sun, the moon, and the stars, and on earth nations will be in dismay, perplexed by the roaring of the sea and the waves. [26] People will die of fright in anticipation of what is coming upon the world, for the powers of the heavens will be shaken. [27] And then they will see the Son of Man coming in a cloud with power and great glory. [28] But when these signs begin to happen, stand erect and raise your heads because your redemption is at hand."

[34] "Beware that your hearts do not become drowsy from carousing and drunkenness and the anxieties of daily life, and that day catch you by surprise [35] like a trap. For that day will assault everyone who lives on the face of the earth. [36] Be vigilant at all times and pray that you have the strength to escape the tribulations that are imminent and to stand before the Son of Man."

Sunday December 8, 2024
Second Sunday of Advent, Year C
First Reading: Baruch 5:1-9

[1] Jerusalem, take off your robe of mourning
and misery;
put on the splendor of glory from God
forever:
[2] Wrapped in the mantle of justice from God,
bear on your head the mitre
that displays the glory of the eternal
name.
[3] For God will show all the earth your
splendor:
[4] you will be named by God forever
the peace of justice, the glory of God's worship.

⁵ Up, Jerusalem! stand upon the heights;
    look to the east and see your children
gathered from the east and the west
     at the word of the Holy One,
     rejoicing that they are remembered by
            God.
⁶ Led away on foot by their enemies they left
           you:
     but God will bring them back to you
     borne aloft in glory as on royal thrones.
⁷ For God has commanded
     that every lofty mountain be made low,
     and the age-old depths and gorges,
     be filled to level ground,
     that Israel may advance secure in the
          glory of God.
⁸ The forests and every kind of fragrant tree
     have overshadowed Israel at God's
          command;
⁹ for God is leading Israel in joy
     by the light of his glory,
     with the mercy and justice for company.

Responsorial Psalm: Psalms 126:1-2, 2-3, 4-5, 6

R. ⁽³⁾ *The Lord has done great things for us; we*
        are filled with joy.

¹ When the LORD brought back the captives of
        Zion,
    we thought we were dreaming.
^{2AB} Then our mouths were filled with laughter;
    and our tongue with rejoicing.
^{2BC} Then they said among the nations,
    "The LORD had done great things for
them."
³ The Lord has done great things for us;
    we are glad indeed.

R. The Lord has done great things for us; we are
       filled with joy.

⁴ Restore our fortunes, O LORD,
    like the torrents in the southern desert.
⁵ Those who sow in tears
    shall reap rejoicing.

R. The Lord has done great things for us; we are
       filled with joy.

⁶ Although they go forth weeping,

carrying the seed to be sown,
they shall some back rejoicing,
   carrying their sheaves.

**R. The Lord has done great things for us; we are
       filled with joy.**

Second Reading: Philippians 1:4-6, 8-11

Brothers and sisters: [4] I pray always with joy in my every prayer for all of you, [5] because of your partnership for the gospel from the first day until now. [6] I am confident of this, that the one who began a good work in you will continue to complete it until the day of Christ Jesus. [8] For God is my witness, how I long for all of you with the affection of Christ Jesus. [9] And this is my prayer: that your love may increase ever more and more in knowledge and every kind of perception, [10] to discern what is of value, so that you may be pure and blameless for the day of Christ, [11] filled with the fruit of righteousness that comes through Jesus Christ for the glory and praise of God.

Alleluia: Luke 3:4, 6
R. Alleluia, alleluia.
[4] Prepare the way of the Lord, make straight
      his paths:
[6] all flesh shall see the salvation of God.
R. Alleluia, alleluia.

Gospel: Luke 3:1-6

[1] In the fifteenth year of the reign of Tiberius Caesar, when Pontius Pilate was governor of Judea, and Herod was tetrarch of Galilee, and his brother Philip tetrarch of the region of Ituraea and Trachonitis, and Lysanias was tetrarch of Abilene, [2] during the high priesthood of Annas and Caiaphas, the word of God came to John the son of Zechariah in the desert. [3] He went throughout the whole region of the Jordan, proclaiming a baptism of repentance for the forgiveness of sins, [4] as it is written in the book of the words of the prophet Isaiah:

"A voice of one crying out in the desert:
'Prepare the way of the Lord,
   make straight his paths.
[5] *Every valley shall be filled*
   and every mountain and hill shall be made low.
The winding roads shall be made straight,
   and the rough ways made smooth,
[6] *and all flesh shall see the salvation of God.'"*

Sunday December 15, 2024
Third Sunday of Advent, Year C

First Reading: Zephaniah 3:14-18A

[14] Shout for joy, O daughter Zion!
    Sing joyfully, O Israel!
Be glad and exult with all your heart,
    O daughter Jerusalem!
[15] The LORD has removed the judgment against
        you
    he has turned away your enemies;
the King of Israel, the LORD, is in your midst,
    you have no further misfortune to fear.
    [16] On that day, it shall be said to Jerusalem:
    Fear not, O Zion, be not discouraged!
[17] The LORD, your God, is in your midst,
    a mighty savior;
he will rejoice over you with gladness,
    and renew you in his love,
he will sing joyfully because of you,
    [18A] as one sings at festivals.

Responsorial Psalm: Isaiah 12:2-3, 4, 5-6.

**R. [6] Cry out with joy and gladness: for among
    you is the great and Holy One of Israel.**
[2] God indeed is my savior;
    I am confident and unafraid.
My strength and my courage is the LORD,
    and he has been my savior.
[3] With joy you will draw water
    at the fountain of salvation.
**R. Cry out with joy and gladness: for among you
    is the great and Holy One of Israel.**
[4] Give thanks to the LORD, acclaim his name;
    among the nations make known his
        deeds,
    proclaim how exalted is his name.
**R. Cry out with joy and gladness: for among you
    is the great and Holy One of Israel.**
[5] Sing praise to the LORD for his glorious
        achievement;
    let this be known throughout all the
        earth.
[6] Shout with exultation, O city of Zion,
    for great in your midst
    is the Holy One of Israel!
R. Cry out with joy and gladness: for among you

is the great and Holy One of Israel.

Second Reading: Philippians 4:4-7

Brothers and sisters: [4] Rejoice in the Lord always. I shall say it again: rejoice! [5] Your kindness should be known to all. The Lord is near. [6] Have no anxiety at all, but in everything, by prayer and petition, with thanksgiving, make your requests known to God. [7]Then the peace of God that surpasses all understanding will guard your hearts and minds in Christ Jesus.

Alleluia: Isaiah 61:1 (Cited in Luke 4:18)
R. Alleluia, alleluia.
[1] The Spirit of the Lord is upon me,
because he has anointed me
to bring glad tidings to the poor.
R. Alleluia, alleluia.

Gospel: Luke 3:10-18

[10] The crowds asked John the Baptist, "What should we do?" [11] He said to them in reply, "Whoever has two cloaks should share with the person who has none. And whoever has food should do likewise." [12] Even tax collectors came to be baptized and they said to him, "Teacher, what should we do?" [13]He answered them, "Stop collecting more than what is prescribed." [14] Soldiers also asked him, "And what is it that we should do?" He told them, "Do not practice extortion, do not falsely accuse anyone, and be satisfied with your wages."
[15] Now the people were filled with expectation, and all were asking in their hearts whether John might be the Christ. [16] John answered them all, saying, "I am baptizing you with water, but one mightier than I is coming. I am not worthy to loosen the thongs of his sandals. He will baptize you with the Holy Spirit and fire. [17] His winnowing fan is in his hand to clear his threshing floor and to gather the wheat into his barn, but the chaff he will burn with unquenchable fire." [18] Exhorting them in many other ways, he preached good news to the people.

Sunday December 22, 2024
Fourth Sunday of Advent, Year C
First Reading: Micah 5:1-4A

Thus says the LORD:

[1] You, Bethlehem-Ephrathah,
    too small to be among the clans of Judah,
from you shall come forth for me
    one who is to be ruler in Israel;
whose origin is from of old,
    from ancient times.

² Therefore the Lord will give them up,
    until the time
when she who is to give birth has borne,
and the rest of his kindred shall return
    to the children of Israel.
³ He shall stand firm and shepherd his flock
    by the strength of the LORD,
    in the majestic name of the LORD, his God;
and they shall remain, for now his greatness
    shall reach to the ends of the earth;
⁴ᴬ he shall be peace.

Responsorial Psalm: Psalms 80:2-3, 15-16, 18-19.

R. ⁽⁴⁾ Lord, make us turn to you; let us see your
    face and we shall be saved.

² O shepherd of Israel, hearken,
    from your throne upon the cherubim,
        shine forth.
³ Rouse your power,
    and come to save us.

R. Lord, make us turn to you; let us see your face
    and we shall be saved.

¹⁵ Once again, O LORD of hosts,
    look down from heaven, and see;
take care of this vine,
    ¹⁶ and protect what your right hand has
        planted
the son of man whom you yourself made
        strong.

R. Lord, make us turn to you; let us see your face
    and we shall be saved.

¹⁸ May your help be with the man of your right
        hand,
    with the son of man whom you yourself made
        strong.
¹⁹ Then we will no more withdraw from you;
    give us new life, and we will call upon
        your name.

R. Lord, make us turn to you; let us see your face
    and we shall be saved.

Second Reading: Hebrews 10:5-10

Brothers and sisters: ⁵ When Christ came into the world, he said:

"Sacrifice and offering you did not desire,
    but a body you prepared for me;
      [6] in holocausts and sin offerings you took
        no delight.
[7] Then I said, 'As is written of me in the scroll,
    behold, I come to do your will, O God.'"
[8] First he says, "Sacrifices and offerings, holocausts and sin offerings, you neither desired nor delighted in." These are offered according to the law. [9] Then he says, "Behold, I come to do your will." He takes away the first to establish the second. [10] By this "will," we have been consecrated through the offering of the body of Jesus Christ once for all.

Alleluia: Luke 1:38
R. Alleluia, alleluia.
[38] Behold, I am the handmaid of the Lord.
May it be done to me according to your
    word.
R. Alleluia, alleluia.

Gospel: Luke 1:39-45
[39] Mary set out and traveled to the hill country in haste to a town of Judah, [40] where she entered the house of Zechariah and greeted Elizabeth. [41] When Elizabeth heard Mary's greeting, the infant leaped in her womb, and Elizabeth, filled with the Holy Spirit, [42] cried out in a loud voice and said, "Blessed are you among women, and blessed is the fruit of your womb. [43] And how does this happen to me, that the mother of my Lord should come to me? [44] For at the moment the sound of your greeting reached my ears, the infant in my womb leaped for joy. [45] Blessed are you who believed that what was spoken to you by the Lord would be fulfilled."

Sunday December 29, 2024
Feast of the Holy Family of Jesus, Mary and Joseph
First Reading: Sirach 3:2-6, 12-14
[2] God sets a father in honor over his
    children;
    a mother's authority he confirms
      over her sons.
[3] Whoever honors his father atones for
    sins,
    and preserves himself from them.
When he prays, he is heard;
    [4] he stores up riches who reveres his
      mother.
[5] Whoever honors his father is gladdened
    by children,
    and, when he prays, is heard.

[6] Whoever reveres his father will live a
            long life;
        he who obeys his father brings
            comfort to his mother.

[12] My son, take care of your father when
        he is old;
        grieve him not as long as he lives.
[13] Even if his mind fail, be considerate of
            him;
        revile him not all the days of his life;
[14] kindness to a father will not be
            forgotten,
        firmly planted against the debt of
            your sins
—a house raised in justice to you.

Or 1 Samuel 1:20-22, 24-28

[20] In those days Hannah conceived, and at the end of her term bore a son whom she called Samuel, since she had asked the LORD for him. [21] The next time her husband Elkanah was going up with the rest of his household to offer the customary sacrifice to the LORD and to fulfill his vows, [22] Hannah did not go, explaining to her husband, "Once the child is weaned, I will take him to appear before the LORD and to remain there forever; I will offer him as a perpetual nazirite."

[24] Once Samuel was weaned, Hannah brought him up with her, along with a three-year-old bull, an ephah of flour, and a skin of wine, and presented him at the temple of the LORD in Shiloh. [25] After the boy's father had sacrificed the young bull, Hannah, his mother, approached Eli and said:

[26] "Pardon, my lord! As you live, my lord, I am the woman who stood near you here, praying to the LORD. [27] I prayed for this child, and the LORD granted my request. [28] Now I, in turn, give him to the LORD; as long as he lives, he shall be dedicated to the LORD." Hannah left Samuel there.

Responsorial Psalm: Psalms 128:1-2, 3, 4-5.

R. (cf. 1) *Blessed are those who fear the Lord and*
            walk in his ways.
[1] Blessed is everyone who fears the LORD,
        who walks in his ways!
[2] For you shall eat the fruit of your handiwork;
        blessed shall you be, and favored.
R. *Blessed are those who fear the Lord and walk*
            in his ways.
[3] Your wife shall be like a fruitful vine
        in the recesses of your home;

your children like olive plants
    around your table.
**R. Blessed are those who fear the Lord and walk
        in his ways.**
[4] Behold, thus is the man blessed
    who fears the LORD.
[5] The LORD bless you from Zion:
    may you see the prosperity of Jerusalem
    all the days of your life.
**R. Blessed are those who fear the Lord and walk
        in his ways.**

Or Psalms 84:2-3, 5-6, 9-10.
**R. (cf. 5a) Blessed are they who dwell in your
        house, O Lord.**
[2] How lovely is your dwelling place, O LORD of
        hosts!
    [3] My soul yearns and pines for the courts
        of the LORD.
My heart and my flesh cry out for the living
        God.
**R. Blessed are they who dwell in your house, O
        Lord.**
[5] Happy they who dwell in your house!
    Continually they praise you.
[6] Happy the men whose strength you are!
    Their hearts are set upon the pilgrimage.
**R. Blessed are they who dwell in your house, O
        Lord.**
[9] O LORD of hosts, hear our prayer;
    hearken, O God of Jacob!
[10] O God, behold our shield,
    and look upon the face of your anointed.
**R. Blessed are they who dwell in your house, O
        Lord.**

Second Reading: Colossians 3:12-21
Brothers and sisters: [12] Put on, as God's chosen ones, holy and beloved, heartfelt compassion, kindness, humility, gentleness, and patience, [13] bearing with one another and forgiving one another, if one has a grievance against another; as the Lord has forgiven you, so must you also do. [14] And over all these put on love, that is, the bond of perfection. [15] And let the peace of Christ control your hearts, the peace into which you were also called in one body. And be thankful. [16] Let the word of Christ dwell in you richly, as in all wisdom you teach and admonish one another,

singing psalms, hymns, and spiritual songs with gratitude in your hearts to God. [17] And whatever you do, in word or in deed, do everything in the name of the Lord Jesus, giving thanks to God the Father through him.

[18] Wives, be subordinate to your husbands, as is proper in the Lord. [19] Husbands, love your wives, and avoid any bitterness toward them. [20] Children, obey your parents in everything, for this is pleasing to the Lord. [21] Fathers, do not provoke your children, so they may not become discouraged.

Or Colossians 3:12-17

Brothers and sisters: [12] Put on, as God's chosen ones, holy and beloved, heartfelt compassion, kindness, humility, gentleness, and patience, [13] bearing with one another and forgiving one another, if one has a grievance against another; as the Lord has forgiven you, so must you also do. [14] And over all these put on love, that is, the bond of perfection. [15] And let the peace of Christ control your hearts, the peace into which you were also called in one body. And be thankful. [16] Let the word of Christ dwell in you richly, as in all wisdom you teach and admonish one another, singing psalms, hymns, and spiritual songs with gratitude in your hearts to God. [17] And whatever you do, in word or in deed, do everything in the name of the Lord Jesus, giving thanks to God the Father through him.

Or 1 John 3:1-2, 21-24

Beloved: [1] See what love the Father has bestowed on us that we may be called the children of God. And so we are. The reason the world does not know us is that it did not know him. [2] Beloved, we are God's children now; what we shall be has not yet been revealed. We do know that when it is revealed we shall be like him, for we shall see him as he is.

[21] Beloved, if our hearts do not condemn us, we have confidence in God [22] and receive from him whatever we ask, because we keep his commandments and do what pleases him. [23] And his commandment is this: we should believe in the name of his Son, Jesus Christ, and love one another just as he commanded us. [24] Those who keep his commandments remain in him, and he in them, and the way we know that he remains in us is from the Spirit he gave us.

Alleluia: Colossians 3:15A, 16A
R. Alleluia, alleluia.
[15A] Let the peace of Christ control your hearts;
[16A] let the word of Christ dwell in you richly.
R. Alleluia, alleluia.

Or cf. Acts 16:14B
R. Alleluia, alleluia.
[14B] Open our hearts, O Lord,
to listen to the words of your Son.
R. Alleluia, alleluia.

Gospel: Luke 2:41-52

[41] Each year Jesus' parents went to Jerusalem for the feast of Passover, [42] and when he was twelve years old, they went up according to festival custom. [43] After they had completed its days, as they were returning, the boy Jesus remained behind in Jerusalem, but his parents did not know it. [44] Thinking that he was in the caravan, they journeyed for a day and looked for him among their relatives and acquaintances, [45] but not finding him, they returned to Jerusalem to look for him. [46] After three days they found him in the temple, sitting in the midst of the teachers, listening to them and asking them questions, [47] and all who heard him were astounded at his understanding and his answers. [48] When his parents saw him, they were astonished, and his mother said to him, "Son, why have you done this to us? Your father and I have been looking for you with great anxiety." [49] And he said to them, "Why were you looking for me? Did you not know that I must be in my Father's house?" [50] But they did not understand what he said to them. [51] He went down with them and came to Nazareth, and was obedient to them; and his mother kept all these things in her heart. [52] And Jesus advanced in wisdom and age and favor before God and man.

JANUARY 2025
Sunday January 5, 2025
Solemnity of the Epiphany of the Lord

First Reading: Isaiah 60:1-6

[1] Rise up in splendor, Jerusalem! Your light
    has come,
      the glory of the Lord shines upon you.
[2] See, darkness covers the earth,
      and thick clouds cover the peoples;
but upon you the LORD shines,
      and over you appears his glory.
[3] Nations shall walk by your light,
      and kings by your shining radiance.
[4] Raise your eyes and look about;
      they all gather and come to you:
your sons come from afar,
      and your daughters in the arms of their
        nurses.

[5] Then you shall be radiant at what you see,
      your heart shall throb and overflow,
for the riches of the sea shall be emptied out
        before you,

the wealth of nations shall be brought to
	you.
[6]Caravans of camels shall fill you,
	dromedaries from Midian and Ephah;
all from Sheba shall come
	bearing gold and frankincense,
	and proclaiming the praises of the LORD.

Responsorial Psalm: Psalms 72:1-2, 7-8, 10-11, 12-13.

R. [(cf. 11)] *Lord, every nation on earth will adore you.*
[1] O God, with your judgment endow the king,
	and with your justice, the king's son;
[2] He shall govern your people with justice
	and your afflicted ones with judgment.
R. Lord, every nation on earth will adore you.
[7] Justice shall flower in his days,
	and profound peace, till the moon be no
		more.
[8] May he rule from sea to sea,
	and from the River to the ends of the
		earth.
R. Lord, every nation on earth will adore you.
[10] The kings of Tarshish and the Isles shall
		offer gifts;
	the kings of Arabia and Seba shall bring
		tribute.
[11] All kings shall pay him homage,
	all nations shall serve him.
R. Lord, every nation on earth will adore you.
[12] For he shall rescue the poor when he cries
		out,
	and the afflicted when he has no one to
		help him.
[13] He shall have pity for the lowly and the
		poor;
	the lives of the poor he shall save.
R. Lord, every nation on earth will adore you.

Second Reading: Ephesians 3:2-3A, 5-6

Brothers and sisters: [2]You have heard of the stewardship of God's grace that was given to me for your benefit, [3A]namely, that the mystery was made known to me by revelation. [5]It was not made known to people in other generations as it has now been revealed to his holy apostles and prophets by the Spirit: [6]that the Gentiles are coheirs, members of the same body, and copartners in the promise in Christ Jesus through the gospel.

Alleluia: Matthew 2:2
R. Alleluia, alleluia.
[2] We saw his star at its rising
and have come to do him homage.
R. Alleluia, alleluia.

Gospel: Matthew 2:1-12
[1] When Jesus was born in Bethlehem of Judea, in the days of King Herod, behold, magi from the east arrived in Jerusalem, [2] saying, "Where is the newborn king of the Jews? We saw his star at its rising and have come to do him homage." [3] When King Herod heard this, he was greatly troubled, and all Jerusalem with him. [4] Assembling all the chief priests and the scribes of the people, He inquired of them where the Christ was to be born. [5] They said to him, "In Bethlehem of Judea, for thus it has been written through the prophet:
[6] *And you, Bethlehem, land of Judah,*
are by no means least among the rulers of
Judah;
since from you shall come a ruler,
who is to shepherd my people Israel."

[7] Then Herod called the magi secretly and ascertained from them the time of the star's appearance. [8] He sent them to Bethlehem and said, "Go and search diligently for the child. When you have found him, bring me word, that I too may go and do him homage." [9] After their audience with the king they set out. And behold, the star that they had seen at its rising preceded them, until it came and stopped over the place where the child was. [10] They were overjoyed at seeing the star, [11] and on entering the house they saw the child with Mary his mother. They prostrated themselves and did him homage. Then they opened their treasures and offered him gifts of gold, frankincense, and myrrh. [12] And having been warned in a dream not to return to Herod, they departed for their country by another way.

Sunday January 12, 2025
Feast of the Baptism of the Lord
First Reading: Isaiah 42:1-4, 6-7
Thus says the LORD:

[1] Here is my servant whom I uphold,
my chosen one with whom I am
pleased,
upon whom I have put my spirit;

he shall bring forth justice to the
  nations,
[2]not crying out, not shouting,
  not making his voice heard in the
    street.
[3]A bruised reed he shall not break,
  and a smoldering wick he shall not
    quench,
[4]until he establishes justice on the earth;
  the coastlands will wait for his
    teaching.

[6] I, the LORD, have called you for the
  victory of justice,
  I have grasped you by the hand;
I formed you, and set you
  as a covenant of the people,
  a light for the nations,
[7]to open the eyes of the blind,
  to bring out prisoners from
    confinement,
  and from the dungeon, those who
    live in darkness.

Or Isaiah 40:1-5, 9-11

[1]Comfort, give comfort to my people,
  says your God.
[2]Speak tenderly to Jerusalem, and
  proclaim to her
  that her service is at an end,
  her guilt is expiated;
indeed, she has received from the hand
    of the LORD
  double for all her sins.

[3]A voice cries out:
In the desert prepare the way of the
    LORD!
  Make straight in the wasteland a
    highway for our God!
[4]Every valley shall be filled in,
  every mountain and hill shall be
    made low;
the rugged land shall be made a plain,
  the rough country, a broad valley.

^{5}Then the glory of the LORD shall be
    revealed,
    and all people shall see it together;
    for the mouth of the LORD has spoken.

^{9}Go up on to a high mountain,
    Zion, herald of glad tidings;
cry out at the top of your voice,
    Jerusalem, herald of good news!
Fear not to cry out
    and say to the cities of Judah:
    Here is your God!
^{10}Here comes with power
    the Lord GOD,
    who rules by a strong arm;
here is his reward with him,
    his recompense before him.
^{11}Like a shepherd he feeds his flock;
    in his arms he gathers the lambs,
carrying them in his bosom,
    and leading the ewes with care.

Responsorial Psalm: Psalms 104:1B-2, 3-4, 24-25, 27-28, 29-30

R. $^{(1)}$ *O bless the Lord, my soul.*
^{1B} O LORD, my God, you are great indeed!
    You are clothed with majesty and glory,
^{2} robed in light as with a cloak.
    You have spread out the heavens like a
        tent-cloth;
R. *O bless the Lord, my soul.*
^{3}You have constructed your palace upon the
        waters.
    You make the clouds your chariot;
you travel on the wings of the wind.
    ^{4}You make the winds your messengers,
and flaming fire your ministers.
R. *O bless the Lord, my soul.*
^{24} How manifold are your works, O LORD!
    In wisdom you have wrought them all–
    the earth is full of your creatures;
^{25} the sea also, great and wide,
    in which are schools without number
    of living things both small and great.
R. *O bless the Lord, my soul.*
^{27} They look to you to give them food in due

20

time.

²⁸When you give it to them, they gather it;
    when you open your hand, they are filled
        with good things.

R. O bless the Lord, my soul.

²⁹If you take away their breath, they perish
        and return to the dust.
³⁰When you send forth your spirit, they are
        created,
    and you renew the face of the earth.

R. O bless the Lord, my soul.

Second Reading: Acts 10:34-38

³⁴Peter proceeded to speak to those gathered in the house of Cornelius, saying: "In truth, I see that God shows no partiality. ³⁵Rather, in every nation whoever fears him and acts uprightly is acceptable to him. ³⁶You know the word that he sent to the Israelites as he proclaimed peace through Jesus Christ, who is Lord of all, ³⁷what has happened all over Judea, beginning in Galilee after the baptism that John preached, ³⁸how God anointed Jesus of Nazareth with the Holy Spirit and power. He went about doing good and healing all those oppressed by the devil, for God was with him."

Or Titus 2:11-14; 3:4-7

Beloved: ¹¹The grace of God has appeared, saving all ¹²and training us to reject godless ways and worldly desires and to live temperately, justly, and devoutly in this age, ¹³as we await the blessed hope, the appearance of the glory of our great God and savior Jesus Christ, ¹⁴who gave himself for us to deliver us from all lawlessness and to cleanse for himself a people as his own, eager to do what is good.

    ⁴When the kindness and generous love of God our savior appeared, ⁵not because of any righteous deeds we had done but because of his mercy, He saved us through the bath of rebirth and renewal by the Holy Spirit, ⁶whom he richly poured out on us through Jesus Christ our savior, ⁷so that we might be justified by his grace and become heirs in hope of eternal life.

Alleluia: see Luke 3:16

R. Alleluia, alleluia.

¹⁶ John said: One mightier than I is coming;
he will baptize you with the Holy Spirit and
        with fire.

R. Alleluia, alleluia.

Gospel: Luke 3:15-16, 21-22

¹⁵The people were filled with expectation, and all were asking in their hearts whether John might be the Christ. ¹⁶John answered them all, saying, "I am baptizing you with

water, but one mightier than I is coming. I am not worthy to loosen the thongs of his sandals. He will baptize you with the Holy Spirit and fire."

[21]After all the people had been baptized and Jesus also had been baptized and was praying, heaven was opened [22]and the Holy Spirit descended upon him in bodily form like a dove. And a voice came from heaven, "You are my beloved Son; with you I am well pleased."

Second Sunday in Ordinary Time Year C

First Reading: Isaiah 62:1-5

[1]For Zion's sake I will not be silent,
    for Jerusalem's sake I will not be quiet,
until her vindication shines forth like the
      dawn
    and her victory like a burning torch.

[2]Nations shall behold your vindication,
    and all the kings your glory;
you shall be called by a new name
    pronounced by the mouth of the LORD.
[3]You shall be a glorious crown in the hand of
      the LORD,
    a royal diadem held by your God.
[4]No more shall people call you "Forsaken,"
    or your land "Desolate,"
but you shall be called "My Delight,"
    and your land "Espoused."
For the LORD delights in you
    and makes your land his spouse.
[5]As a young man marries a virgin,
    your Builder shall marry you;
and as a bridegroom rejoices in his bride
    so shall your God rejoice in you.

Responsorial Psalm: Psalms 96:1-2, 2-3, 7-8, 9-10

R. [3] *Proclaim his marvelous deeds to all the*
         nations.
[1] Sing to the LORD a new song;
    sing to the LORD, all you lands.
[2A] Sing to the LORD; bless his name.
R. Proclaim his marvelous deeds to all the
         nations.
[2B] Announce his salvation, day after day.
   [3]Tell his glory among the nations;
among all peoples, his wondrous deeds.

*R. Proclaim his marvelous deeds to all the
    nations.*

[7] Give to the LORD, you families of nations,
    give to the LORD glory and praise;
[8A] give to the LORD the glory due his name!

*R. Proclaim his marvelous deeds to all the
    nations.*

[9] Worship the LORD in holy attire.
    Tremble before him, all the earth;
[10] Say among the nations: The LORD is king.
    He governs the peoples with equity.

*R. Proclaim his marvelous deeds to all the
    nations.*

Second Reading: 1 Corinthians 12:4-11

Brothers and sisters: [4]There are different kinds of spiritual gifts but the same Spirit; [5]there are different forms of service but the same Lord; [6]there are different workings but the same God who produces all of them in everyone. [7]To each individual the manifestation of the Spirit is given for some benefit. [8]To one is given through the Spirit the expression of wisdom; to another, the expression of knowledge according to the same Spirit; [9]to another, faith by the same Spirit; to another, gifts of healing by the one Spirit; [10]to another, mighty deeds; to another, prophecy; to another, discernment of spirits; to another, varieties of tongues; to another, interpretation of tongues. [11]But one and the same Spirit produces all of these, distributing them individually to each person as he wishes.

Alleluia: see 2 Thessalonians 2:14

R. Alleluia, alleluia.

[14] God has called us through the Gospel
to possess the glory of our Lord Jesus Christ.

R. Alleluia, alleluia.

Gospel: John 2:1-11

[1]There was a wedding at Cana in Galilee, and the mother of Jesus was there. [2]Jesus and his disciples were also invited to the wedding. [3]When the wine ran short, the mother of Jesus said to him, "They have no wine." [4]And Jesus said to her, "Woman, how does your concern affect me? My hour has not yet come." [5]His mother said to the servers, "Do whatever he tells you." [6]Now there were six stone water jars there for Jewish ceremonial washings, each holding twenty to thirty gallons. [7]Jesus told the them, "Fill the jars with water." So they filled them to the brim. [8]Then he told them, "Draw some out now and take it to the headwaiter." So they took it. [9]And when the headwaiter tasted the water that had become wine, without knowing where it came from —although the servers who had drawn the water knew,— the headwaiter called the bridegroom [10]and said to him, "Everyone serves good wine first, and then when

people have drunk freely, an inferior one; but you have kept the good wine until now." [11]Jesus did this as the beginning of his signs at Cana in Galilee and so revealed his glory, and his disciples began to believe in him.

Sunday January 26, 2025
Third Sunday in Ordinary Time, Year C
First Reading: Nehemiah 8:2-4A, 5-6, 8-10

[2]Ezra the priest brought the law before the assembly, which consisted of men, women, and those children old enough to understand. [3]Standing at one end of the open place that was before the Water Gate, he read out of the book from daybreak till midday, in the presence of the men, the women, and those children old enough to understand; and all the people listened attentively to the book of the law. [4A]Ezra the scribe stood on a wooden platform that had been made for the occasion. [5]He opened the scroll so that all the people might see it —for he was standing higher up than any of the people—; and, as he opened it, all the people rose. [6]Ezra blessed the LORD, the great God, and all the people, their hands raised high, answered, "Amen, amen!" Then they bowed down and prostrated themselves before the LORD, their faces to the ground. [8]Ezra read plainly from the book of the law of God, interpreting it so that all could understand what was read. [9]Then Nehemiah, that is, His Excellency, and Ezra the priest-scribe and the Levites who were instructing the people said to all the people: "Today is holy to the LORD your God. Do not be sad, and do not weep"— for all the people were weeping as they heard the words of the law. [10]He said further: "Go, eat rich foods and drink sweet drinks, and allot portions to those who had nothing prepared; for today is holy to our LORD. Do not be saddened this day, for rejoicing in the LORD must be your strength!"

Responsorial Psalm: Psalms 19:8, 9, 10, 15

R. (cf John 6:63c) *Your words, Lord, are Spirit and life.*

[8] The law of the LORD is perfect,
     refreshing the soul;
The decree of the LORD is trustworthy,
     giving wisdom to the simple.

R. Your words, Lord, are Spirit and life.

[9] The precepts of the LORD are right,
     rejoicing the heart;
The command of the LORD is clear,
     enlightening the eye.

R. Your words, Lord, are Spirit and life.

[10] The fear of the LORD is pure,
     enduring forever;
The ordinances of the LORD are true,

all of them just.

R. Your words, Lord, are Spirit and life.

[15] Let the words of my mouth and the thought
     of my heart
    find favor before you,
O LORD, my rock and my redeemer.

R. Your words, Lord, are Spirit and life.

Second Reading: 1 Corinthians 12:12-30

Brothers and sisters: [12]As a body is one though it has many parts, and all the parts of the body, though many, are one body, so also Christ. [13]For in one Spirit we were all baptized into one body, whether Jews or Greeks, slaves or free persons, and we were all given to drink of one Spirit.

    [14]Now the body is not a single part, but many. [15]If a foot should say, "Because I am not a hand I do not belong to the body," it does not for this reason belong any less to the body. [16]Or if an ear should say, "Because I am not an eye I do not belong to the body," it does not for this reason belong any less to the body. [17]If the whole body were an eye, where would the hearing be? If the whole body were hearing, where would the sense of smell be? [18]But as it is, God placed the parts, each one of them, in the body as he intended. [19]If they were all one part, where would the body be? [20]But as it is, there are many parts, yet one body. [21]The eye cannot say to the hand, "I do not need you," nor again the head to the feet, "I do not need you." [22]Indeed, the parts of the body that seem to be weaker are all the more necessary, [23]and those parts of the body that we consider less honorable we surround with greater honor, and our less presentable parts are treated with greater propriety, [24]whereas our more presentable parts do not need this. But God has so constructed the body as to give greater honor to a part that is without it, [25]so that there may be no division in the body, but that the parts may have the same concern for one another. [26]If one part suffers, all the parts suffer with it; if one part is honored, all the parts share its joy.

    [27]Now you are Christ's body, and individually parts of it. [28]Some people God has designated in the church to be, first, apostles; second, prophets; third, teachers; then, mighty deeds; then gifts of healing, assistance, administration, and varieties of tongues. [29]Are all apostles? Are all prophets? Are all teachers? Do all work mighty deeds? [30]Do all have gifts of healing? Do all speak in tongues? Do all interpret?

Or 1 Corinthians 12:12-14, 27

Brothers and sisters: [12]As a body is one though it has many parts, and all the parts of the body, though many, are one body, so also Christ. [13]For in one Spirit we were all baptized into one body, whether Jews or Greeks, slaves or free persons, and we were all given to drink of one Spirit. [14]Now the body is not a single part, but many. [27]Now you are Christ's body, and individually parts of it.

Alleluia: Luke 4:18

R. Alleluia, alleluia.
[18] The Lord sent me to bring glad tidings to the
        poor,
and to proclaim liberty to captives.
R. Alleluia, alleluia.

Gospel: Luke 1:1-4; 4:14-21

[1]Since many have undertaken to compile a narrative of the events that have been fulfilled among us, [2]just as those who were eyewitnesses from the beginning and ministers of the word have handed them down to us, [3]I too have decided, after investigating everything accurately anew, to write it down in an orderly sequence for you, most excellent Theophilus, [4]so that you may realize the certainty of the teachings you have received.

   [14]Jesus returned to Galilee in the power of the Spirit, and news of him spread throughout the whole region. [15]He taught in their synagogues and was praised by all.

   [16]He came to Nazareth, where he had grown up, and went according to his custom into the synagogue on the sabbath day. He stood up to read [17]and was handed a scroll of the prophet Isaiah. He unrolled the scroll and found the passage where it was written:

[18]*The Spirit of the Lord is upon me,*
    because he has anointed me
    to bring glad tidings to the poor.
He has sent me to proclaim liberty to captives
    and recovery of sight to the blind,
    to let the oppressed go free,
    [19]*and to proclaim a year acceptable to the*
        Lord.

[20]Rolling up the scroll, he handed it back to the attendant and sat down, and the eyes of all in the synagogue looked intently at him. [21]He said to them, "Today this Scripture passage is fulfilled in your hearing."

FEBRUARY 2025
Sunday February 2, 2025
Feast of the Presentation of the Lord

First Reading: Malachi 3:1-4

  [1] Thus says the Lord GOD:
Lo, I am sending my messenger
   to prepare the way before me;
And suddenly there will come to the temple

the LORD whom you seek,
And the messenger of the covenant whom
you desire.
Yes, he is coming, says the LORD of hosts.
[2] But who will endure the day of his coming?
And who can stand when he appears?
For he is like the refiner's fire,
or like the fuller's lye.
[3] He will sit refining and purifying silver,
and he will purify the sons of Levi,
Refining them like gold or like silver
that they may offer due sacrifice to the
LORD.
[4] Then the sacrifice of Judah and Jerusalem
will please the LORD,
as in the days of old, as in years gone by.

Responsorial Psalm: Psalms 24:7, 8, 9, 10
R. [8] *Who is this king of glory? It is the Lord!*
[7] Lift up, O gates, your lintels;
reach up, you ancient portals,
that the king of glory may come in!
R. Who is this king of glory? It is the Lord!
[8] Who is this king of glory?
The LORD, strong and mighty,
the LORD, mighty in battle.
R. Who is this king of glory? It is the Lord!
[9] Lift up, O gates, your lintels;
reach up, you ancient portals,
that the king of glory may come in!
R. Who is this king of glory? It is the Lord!
[10] Who is this king of glory?
The LORD of hosts; he is the king of glory.
R. Who is this king of glory? It is the Lord!

Second Reading: Hebrews 2:14-18
[14] Since the children share in blood and flesh, Jesus likewise shared in them, that through death he might destroy the one who has the power of death, that is, the Devil, [15] and free those who through fear of death had been subject to slavery all their life. [16] Surely he did not help angels but rather the descendants of Abraham; [17] therefore, he had to become like his brothers and sisters in every way, that he might be a merciful and faithful high priest before God to expiate the sins of the people. [18] Because he himself was tested through what he suffered, he is able to help those who are being tested.

Alleluia: Luke 2:32
R. Alleluia, alleluia.
[32] A light of revelation to the Gentiles,
and glory for your people Israel.
R. Alleluia, alleluia.

Gospel: Luke 2:22-40

[22] When the days were completed for their purification according to the law of Moses, Mary and Joseph took Jesus up to Jerusalem to present him to the Lord, [23] just as it is written in the law of the Lord, *Every male that opens the womb shall be consecrated to the Lord*, [24] and to offer the sacrifice of *a pair of turtledoves or two young pigeons*, in accordance with the dictate in the law of the Lord.

[25] Now there was a man in Jerusalem whose name was Simeon. This man was righteous and devout, awaiting the consolation of Israel, and the Holy Spirit was upon him. [26] It had been revealed to him by the Holy Spirit that he should not see death before he had seen the Christ of the Lord. [27] He came in the Spirit into the temple; and when the parents brought in the child Jesus to perform the custom of the law in regard to him, [28] he took him into his arms and blessed God, saying:
[29] "Now, Master, you may let your servant
         go
     in peace, according to your word,
[30] for my eyes have seen your salvation,
     [31] which you prepared in the sight of all
         the peoples:
[32] a light for revelation to the Gentiles,
     and glory for your people Israel."
[33] The child's father and mother were amazed at what was said about him; [34] and Simeon blessed them and said to Mary his mother, "Behold, this child is destined for the fall and rise of many in Israel, and to be a sign that will be contradicted [35] — and you yourself a sword will pierce— so that the thoughts of many hearts may be revealed." [36] There was also a prophetess, Anna, the daughter of Phanuel, of the tribe of Asher. She was advanced in years, having lived seven years with her husband after her marriage, [37] and then as a widow until she was eighty-four. She never left the temple, but worshiped night and day with fasting and prayer. [38]And coming forward at that very time, she gave thanks to God and spoke about the child to all who were awaiting the redemption of Jerusalem.

[39] When they had fulfilled all the prescriptions of the law of the Lord, they returned to Galilee, to their own town of Nazareth. [40] The child grew and became strong, filled with wisdom; and the favor of God was upon him.

Or Luke 2:22-32

22 When the days were completed for their purification according to the law of Moses, Mary and Joseph took Jesus up to Jerusalem to present him to the Lord, 23 just as it is written in the law of the Lord, *Every male that opens the womb shall be consecrated to the Lord,* 24 and to offer the sacrifice of *a pair of turtledoves or two young pigeons*, in accordance with the dictate in the law of the Lord.

25 Now there was a man in Jerusalem whose name was Simeon. This man was righteous and devout, awaiting the consolation of Israel, and the Holy Spirit was upon him. 26It had been revealed to him by the Holy Spirit that he should not see death before he had seen the Christ of the Lord. 27He came in the Spirit into the temple; and when the parents brought in the child Jesus to perform the custom of the law in regard to him, 28he took him into his arms and blessed God, saying:
29 "Now, Master, you may let your servant
      go
   in peace, according to your word,
30 for my eyes have seen your salvation,
    31 which you prepared in the sight of all
      the peoples:
32 a light for revelation to the Gentiles,
   and glory for your people Israel."

Sunday February 9, 2025

Fifth Sunday in Ordinary Time Year C

First Reading: Isaiah 6:1-2A, 3-8

1In the year King Uzziah died, I saw the Lord seated on a high and lofty throne, with the train of his garment filling the temple. 2ASeraphim were stationed above.

3They cried one to the other, "Holy, holy, holy is the LORD of hosts! All the earth is filled with his glory!" 4At the sound of that cry, the frame of the door shook and the house was filled with smoke.

5Then I said, "Woe is me, I am doomed! For I am a man of unclean lips, living among a people of unclean lips; yet my eyes have seen the King, the LORD of hosts!" 6Then one of the seraphim flew to me, holding an ember that he had taken with tongs from the altar.

7He touched my mouth with it, and said, "See, now that this has touched your lips, your wickedness is removed, your sin purged."

8Then I heard the voice of the Lord saying, "Whom shall I send? Who will go for us?" "Here I am," I said; "send me!"

Responsorial Psalm: Psalms 138:1-2, 2-3, 4-5, 7-8

R. (1c) *In the sight of the angels I will sing your*
      praises, Lord.
1I will give thanks to you, O LORD, with all my
    heart,
   for you have heard the words of my
     mouth;
   in the presence of the angels I will sing

29

your praise;
²ᴬᴮ I will worship at your holy temple
and give thanks to your name.

R. In the sight of the angels I will sing your praises, Lord.

²ᴮᶜ Because of your kindness and your truth;
for you have made great above all things
your name and your promise.
³ When I called, you answered me;
you built up strength within me.

R. In the sight of the angels I will sing your praises, Lord.

⁴All the kings of the earth shall give thanks to
you, O LORD,
when they hear the words of your mouth;
⁵ and they shall sing of the ways of the LORD:
"Great is the glory of the LORD."

R. In the sight of the angels I will sing your praises, Lord.

⁷ᴰYour right hand saves me.
⁸The LORD will complete what he has done
for me;
your kindness, O LORD, endures forever;
forsake not the work of your hands.

R. In the sight of the angels I will sing your praises, Lord.

Second Reading: 1 Corinthians 15:1-11

¹I am reminding you, brothers and sisters, of the gospel I preached to you, which you indeed received and in which you also stand. ²Through it you are also being saved, if you hold fast to the word I preached to you, unless you believed in vain. ³For I handed on to you as of first importance what I also received: that Christ died for our sins in accordance with the Scriptures; ⁴that he was buried; that he was raised on the third day in accordance with the Scriptures; ⁵that he appeared to Cephas, then to the Twelve. ⁶After that, Christ appeared to more than five hundred brothers at once, most of whom are still living, though some have fallen asleep. ⁷After that he appeared to James, then to all the apostles. ⁸Last of all, as to one born abnormally, he appeared to me. ⁹For I am the least of the apostles, not fit to be called an apostle, because I persecuted the church of God. ¹⁰But by the grace of God I am what I am, and his grace to me has not been ineffective. Indeed, I have toiled harder than all of them; not I, however, but the grace of God that is with me. ¹¹Therefore, whether it be I or they, so we preach and so you believed.

Or 1 Corinthians 15:3-8, 11

Brothers and sisters, [3]For I handed on to you as of first importance what I also received: that Christ died for our sins in accordance with the Scriptures; [4]that he was buried; that he was raised on the third day in accordance with the Scriptures; [5]that he appeared to Cephas, then to the Twelve. [6]After that, he appeared to more than five hundred brothers at once, most of whom are still living, though some have fallen asleep. [7]After that he appeared to James, then to all the apostles. [8]Last of all, as to one abnormally born, he appeared to me. [11]Therefore, whether it be I or they, so we preach and so you believed.

Alleluia: Matthew 4:19
R. Alleluia, alleluia.
[19] Come after me
and I will make you fishers of men.
R. Alleluia, alleluia.

Gospel: Luke 5:1-11
[1]While the crowd was pressing in on Jesus and listening to the word of God, he was standing by the Lake of Gennesaret. [2]He saw two boats there alongside the lake; the fishermen had disembarked and were washing their nets. [3]Getting into one of the boats, the one belonging to Simon, he asked him to put out a short distance from the shore. Then he sat down and taught the crowds from the boat. [4]After he had finished speaking, he said to Simon, "Put out into deep water and lower your nets for a catch." [5]Simon said in reply, "Master, we have worked hard all night and have caught nothing, but at your command I will lower the nets." [6]When they had done this, they caught a great number of fish and their nets were tearing. [7]They signaled to their partners in the other boat to come to help them.
They came and filled both boats so that the boats were in danger of sinking. [8]When Simon Peter saw this, he fell at the knees of Jesus and said, "Depart from me, Lord, for I am a sinful man." [9]For astonishment at the catch of fish they had made seized him and all those with him, [10]and likewise James and John, the sons of Zebedee, who were partners of Simon. Jesus said to Simon, "Do not be afraid; from now on you will be catching men." [11]When they brought their boats to the shore, they left everything and followed him.

Sunday February 16, 2025
Sixth Sunday in Ordinary Time Year C
First Reading: Jeremiah 17:5-8
[5]Thus says the LORD:

Cursed is the one who trusts in human
    beings,
  who seeks his strength in flesh,
  whose heart turns away from the LORD.
[6]He is like a barren bush in the desert
  that enjoys no change of season,

but stands in a lava waste,
    a salt and empty earth.
    [7]Blessed is the one who trusts in the LORD,
    whose hope is the LORD.
[8]He is like a tree planted beside the waters
    that stretches out its roots to the stream:
It fears not the heat when it comes;
    its leaves stay green;
in the year of drought it shows no distress,
    but still bears fruit.

Responsorial Psalm: Psalms 1:1-2, 3, 4 AND 6

R. [40:5a] ***Blessed are they who hope in the Lord.***
[1]Blessed the man who follows not
    the counsel of the wicked,
nor walks in the way of sinners,
    nor sits in the company of the insolent,
[2] but delights in the law of the LORD
    and meditates on his law day and night.
R. Blessed are they who hope in the Lord.
[3]He is like a tree
    planted near running water,
that yields its fruit in due season,
    and whose leaves never fade.
    Whatever he does, prospers.
R. Blessed are they who hope in the Lord.
[4] Not so the wicked, not so;
    they are like chaff which the wind drives
      away.
[6] For the LORD watches over the way of the
      just,
    but the way of the wicked vanishes.
R. Blessed are they who hope in the Lord.

Second Reading: 1 Corinthians 15:12, 16-20

Brothers and sisters: [12]If Christ is preached as raised from the dead, how can some among you say there is no resurrection of the dead? [16]If the dead are not raised, neither has Christ been raised, [17]and if Christ has not been raised, your faith is vain; you are still in your sins. [18]Then those who have fallen asleep in Christ have perished. [19]If for this life only we have hoped in Christ, we are the most pitiable people of all.

    [20]But now Christ has been raised from the dead, the firstfruits of those who have fallen asleep.

Alleluia: Luke 6:23AB
R. Alleluia, alleluia.
23AB Rejoice and be glad;
your reward will be great in heaven.
R. Alleluia, alleluia.

Gospel: Luke 6:17, 20-26
17 Jesus came down with the Twelve and stood on a stretch of level ground with a great crowd of his disciples and a large number of the people from all Judea and Jerusalem and the coastal region of Tyre and Sidon. 20 And raising his eyes toward his disciples he said:

"Blessed are you who are poor,
    for the kingdom of God is yours.
21 Blessed are you who are now hungry,
    for you will be satisfied.
Blessed are you who are now weeping,
    for you will laugh.
22 Blessed are you when people hate you,
    and when they exclude and insult you,
    and denounce your name as evil
    on account of the Son of Man.

23 Rejoice and leap for joy on that day! Behold, your reward will be great in heaven. For their ancestors treated the prophets in the same way.

24 But woe to you who are rich,
    for you have received your consolation.
25 Woe to you who are filled now,
    for you will be hungry.
Woe to you who laugh now,
    for you will grieve and weep.
26 Woe to you when all speak well of you,
    for their ancestors treated the false
        prophets in this way."

Sunday February 23, 2025
Seventh Sunday in Ordinary Time, Year C
First Reading: 1 Samuel 26:2,7-9,12-13, 22-23
2 In those days, Saul went down to the desert of Ziph with three thousand picked men of Israel, to search for David in the desert of Ziph. 7 So David and Abishai went among Saul's soldiers by night and found Saul lying asleep within the barricade, with his spear thrust into the ground at his head and Abner and his men sleeping around him.

[8]Abishai whispered to David: "God has delivered your enemy into your grasp this day. Let me nail him to the ground with one thrust of the spear; I will not need a second thrust!" [9]But David said to Abishai, "Do not harm him, for who can lay hands on the LORD's anointed and remain unpunished?" [12]So David took the spear and the water jug from their place at Saul's head, and they got away without anyone's seeing or knowing or awakening. All remained asleep, because the LORD had put them into a deep slumber.

[13]Going across to an opposite slope, David stood on a remote hilltop at a great distance from Abner, son of Ner, and the troops. [22]He said: "Here is the king's spear. Let an attendant come over to get it. [23]The LORD will reward each man for his justice and faithfulness. Today, though the LORD delivered you into my grasp, I would not harm the LORD's anointed."

Responsorial Psalm: Psalms 103:1-2, 3-4, 8, 10, 12-13

R. [8a] *The Lord is kind and merciful.*

[1] Bless the LORD, O my soul;
    and all my being, bless his holy name.
[2] Bless the LORD, O my soul,
    and forget not all his benefits.

R. *The Lord is kind and merciful.*

[2] He pardons all your iniquities,
    heals all your ills.
[4] He redeems your life from destruction,
    crowns you with kindness and
        compassion.

R. *The Lord is kind and merciful.*

[8] Merciful and gracious is the LORD,
    slow to anger and abounding in
        kindness.
[10] Not according to our sins does he deal with
        us,
    nor does he requite us according to our
        crimes.

R. *The Lord is kind and merciful.*

[12] As far as the east is from the west,
    so far has he put our transgressions from
        us.
[13] As a father has compassion on his children,
    so the LORD has compassion on those who
        fear him.

R. *The Lord is kind and merciful.*

Second Reading: 1 Corinthians 15:45-49

Brothers and sisters: ⁴⁵It is written, *The first man, Adam, became a living being*, the last Adam a life-giving spirit. ⁴⁶But the spiritual was not first; rather the natural and then the spiritual. ⁴⁷The first man was from the earth, earthly; the second man, from heaven. ⁴⁸As was the earthly one, so also are the earthly, and as is the heavenly one, so also are the heavenly. ⁴⁹Just as we have borne the image of the earthly one, we shall also bear the image of the heavenly one.

Alleluia: John 13:34
R. Alleluia, alleluia.
³⁴ I give you a new commandment, says the
        Lord:
Love one another as I have loved you.
R. Alleluia, alleluia.

Gospel: Luke 6:27-38
Jesus said to his disciples: ²⁷"To you who hear I say, love your enemies, do good to those who hate you, ²⁸bless those who curse you, pray for those who mistreat you. ²⁹To the person who strikes you on one cheek, offer the other one as well, and from the person who takes your cloak, do not withhold even your tunic. ³⁰Give to everyone who asks of you, and from the one who takes what is yours do not demand it back. ³¹Do to others as you would have them do to you. ³²For if you love those who love you, what credit is that to you? Even sinners love those who love them. ³³And if you do good to those who do good to you, what credit is that to you? Even sinners do the same. ³⁴If you lend money to those from whom you expect repayment, what credit is that to you? Even sinners lend to sinners, and get back the same amount. ³⁵But rather, love your enemies and do good to them, and lend expecting nothing back; then your reward will be great and you will be children of the Most High, for he himself is kind to the ungrateful and the wicked. ³⁶Be merciful, just as your Father is merciful.
    ³⁷"Stop judging and you will not be judged. Stop condemning and you will not be condemned. Forgive and you will be forgiven. ³⁸Give, and gifts will be given to you; a good measure, packed together, shaken down, and overflowing, will be poured into your lap. For the measure with which you measure will in return be measured out to you."

MARCH 2025

Sunday March 2, 2025

Eighth Sunday in Ordinary Time, Year C
First Reading: Sirach 27:4-7
⁴When a sieve is shaken, the husks appear;
      so do one's faults when one speaks.
⁵ As the test of what the potter molds is in the
        furnace,
      so in tribulation is the test of the just.

⁶ The fruit of a tree shows the care it has had;
  so too does one's speech disclose the bent
   of one's mind.
⁷ Praise no one before he speaks,
  for it is then that people are tested.

Responsorial Psalm: Psalms 92:2-3, 13-14, 15-16

R. *(cf. 2a)* **Lord, it is good to give thanks to you.**
² It is good to give thanks to the LORD,
  to sing praise to your name, Most High,
³ To proclaim your kindness at dawn
  and your faithfulness throughout the
   night.
R. Lord, it is good to give thanks to you.
¹³ The just one shall flourish like the palm tree,
  like a cedar of Lebanon shall he grow.
¹⁴ They that are planted in the house of the
   LORD
  shall flourish in the courts of our God.
R. Lord, it is good to give thanks to you.
¹⁵ They shall bear fruit even in old age;
  vigorous and sturdy shall they be,
¹⁶ Declaring how just is the LORD,
  my rock, in whom there is no wrong.
R. Lord, it is good to give thanks to you.

Second Reading: 1 Corinthians 15:54-58

Brothers and sisters: ⁵⁴When this which is corruptible clothes itself with incorruptibility and this which is mortal clothes itself with immortality, then the word that is written shall come about:

Death is swallowed up in victory.
⁵⁵*Where, O death, is your victory?*
Where, O death, is your sting?
⁵⁶The sting of death is sin, and the power of sin is the law. ⁵⁷But thanks be to God who gives us the victory through our Lord Jesus Christ.

 ⁵⁸Therefore, my beloved brothers and sisters, be firm, steadfast, always fully devoted to the work of the Lord, knowing that in the Lord your labor is not in vain.

Alleluia: Philippians 2:15D, 16A

R. Alleluia, alleluia.
^{15D} Shine like lights in the world
^{16A} as you hold on to the word of life.
R. Alleluia, alleluia.

Gospel: Luke 6:39-45

[39]Jesus told his disciples a parable, "Can a blind person guide a blind person? Will not both fall into a pit? [40]No disciple is superior to the teacher; but when fully trained, every disciple will be like his teacher. [41]Why do you notice the splinter in your brother's eye, but do not perceive the wooden beam in your own? [42]How can you say to your brother, 'Brother, let me remove that splinter in your eye,' when you do not even notice the wooden beam in your own eye? You hypocrite! Remove the wooden beam from your eye first; then you will see clearly to remove the splinter in your brother's eye.

[43]"A good tree does not bear rotten fruit, nor does a rotten tree bear good fruit. [44]For every tree is known by its own fruit. For people do not pick figs from thornbushes, nor do they gather grapes from brambles. [45]A good person out of the store of goodness in his heart produces good, but an evil person out of a store of evil produces evil; for from the fullness of the heart the mouth speaks."

Sunday March 9, 2025

First Sunday of Lent, Year C

First Reading: Deuteronomy 26:4-10

Moses spoke to the people, saying: [4]"The priest shall receive the basket from you and shall set it in front of the altar of the LORD, your God. [5]Then you shall declare before the LORD, your God, 'My father was a wandering Aramean who went down to Egypt with a small household and lived there as an alien. But there he became a nation great, strong, and numerous. [6]When the Egyptians maltreated and oppressed us, imposing hard labor upon us, [7]we cried to the LORD, the God of our fathers, and he heard our cry and saw our affliction, our toil, and our oppression. [8]He brought us out of Egypt with his strong hand and outstretched arm, with terrifying power, with signs and wonders; [9]and bringing us into this country, he gave us this land flowing with milk and honey. [10]Therefore, I have now brought you the firstfruits of the products of the soil which you, O LORD, have given me.' And having set them before the LORD, your God, you shall bow down in his presence."

Responsorial Psalm: Psalms 91:1-2, 10-11, 12-13, 14-15.

R. (cf. 15b) *Be with me, Lord, when I am in trouble.*

[1] You who dwell in the shelter of the Most
      High,
   who abide in the shadow of the Almighty,
[2] say to the LORD, "My refuge and fortress,
   my God in whom I trust."

R. *Be with me, Lord, when I am in trouble.*

[10] No evil shall befall you,
   nor shall affliction come near your tent,
[11] For to his angels he has given command
      about you,
   that they guard you in all your ways.

R. Be with me, Lord, when I am in trouble.
[12] Upon their hands they shall bear you up,
    lest you dash your foot against a stone.
[13] You shall tread upon the asp and the viper;
    you shall trample down the lion and the
        dragon.
R. Be with me, Lord, when I am in trouble.
[14] Because he clings to me, I will deliver him;
    I will set him on high because he
        acknowledges my name.
[15] He shall call upon me, and I will answer
        him;
    I will be with him in distress;
I will deliver him and glorify him.
R. Be with me, Lord, when I am in trouble.

Second Reading: Romans 10:8-13

Brothers and sisters: [8]What does Scripture say?

The word is near you,
    in your mouth and in your heart

—that is, the word of faith that we preach—, [9]for, if you confess with your mouth that Jesus is Lord and believe in your heart that God raised him from the dead, you will be saved. [10]For one believes with the heart and so is justified, and one confesses with the mouth and so is saved. [11]For the Scripture says,

No one who believes in him will be put to
    shame.

[12]For there is no distinction between Jew and Greek; the same Lord is Lord of all, enriching all who call upon him. [13]For "everyone who calls on the name of the Lord will be saved."

Verse before the Gospel: Matthew 4:4B

[4B] One does not live on bread alone,
but on every word that comes forth from the
    mouth of God.

Gospel: Luke 4:1-13

[1]Filled with the Holy Spirit, Jesus returned from the Jordan and was led by the Spirit into the desert [2]for forty days, to be tempted by the devil. He ate nothing during those days and when they were over he was hungry. [3]The devil said to him,

"If you are the Son of God, command this stone to become bread." [4]Jesus answered him, "It is written, *One does not live on bread alone*." [5]Then he took him up and showed him all the kingdoms of the world in a single instant. [6]The devil said to him, "I shall give to you all this power and glory; for it has been handed over to me, and I may give it to whomever I wish. [7]All this will be yours, if you worship me." [8]Jesus said to him in reply, "It is written:

You shall worship the Lord, your God,
and him alone shall you serve."

[9] Then he led him to Jerusalem, made him stand on the parapet of the temple, and said to him, "If you are the Son of God, throw yourself down from here, [10]for it is written:

He will command his angels concerning you,
to guard you,

[11]and:

With their hands they will support you,
lest you dash your foot against a stone."

[12] Jesus said to him in reply, "It also says,

You shall not put the Lord, your God, to the
test."

[13] When the devil had finished every temptation, he departed from him for a time.

Sunday March 16, 2025

Second Sunday of Lent, Year C

First Reading: Genesis 15:5-12, 17-18

[5]The Lord God took Abram outside and said, "Look up at the sky and count the stars, if you can. Just so," he added, "shall your descendants be." [6]Abram put his faith in the LORD, who credited it to him as an act of righteousness.

[7]He then said to him, "I am the LORD who brought you from Ur of the Chaldeans to give you this land as a possession." [8]"O Lord GOD," he asked, "how am I to know that I shall possess it?" [9]He answered him, "Bring me a three-year-old heifer, a three-year-old she-goat, a three-year-old ram, a turtledove, and a young pigeon." [10]Abram brought him all these, split them in two, and placed each half opposite the other; but the birds he did not cut up. [11]Birds of prey swooped down on the carcasses, but Abram stayed with them. [12]As the sun was about to set, a trance fell upon Abram, and a deep, terrifying darkness enveloped him.

[17]When the sun had set and it was dark, there appeared a smoking fire pot and a flaming torch, which passed between those pieces. [18]It was on that occasion that the LORD made a covenant with Abram, saying: "To your descendants I give this land, from the Wadi of Egypt to the Great River, the Euphrates."

Responsorial Psalm: Psalms 27:1, 7-8, 8-9, 13-14.

R. *[1a]* ***The Lord is my light and my salvation.***

[1]The LORD is my light and my salvation;

whom should I fear?

The LORD is my life's refuge;

of whom should I be afraid?

R. *The Lord is my light and my salvation.*

[7]Hear, O LORD, the sound of my call;

have pity on me, and answer me.

[8A] Of you my heart speaks; you my glance

seeks.

R. *The Lord is my light and my salvation.*

[8B] Your presence, O LORD, I seek.

[9]Hide not your face from me;

do not in anger repel your servant.

You are my helper: cast me not off.

R. *The Lord is my light and my salvation.*

[13] I believe that I shall see the bounty of the

LORD

in the land of the living.

[14] Wait for the LORD with courage;

be stouthearted, and wait for the LORD.

R. *The Lord is my light and my salvation.*

Second Reading: Philippians 3:17-4:1

[17]Join with others in being imitators of me, brothers and sisters, and observe those who thus conduct themselves according to the model you have in us. [18]For many,

as I have often told you and now tell you even in tears, conduct themselves as enemies of the cross of Christ. [19]Their end is destruction. Their God is their stomach; their glory is in their "shame." Their minds are occupied with earthly things. [20]But our citizenship is in heaven, and from it, we also await a savior, the Lord Jesus Christ. [21]He will change our lowly body to conform with his glorified body by the power that enables him also to bring all things into subjection to himself.

[1]Therefore, my brothers and sisters, whom I love and long for, my joy and crown, in this way stand firm in the Lord.

Or Philippians 3:20-4:1

Brothers and sisters: [20]But our citizenship is in heaven, and from it we also await a savior, the Lord Jesus Christ. [21]He will change our lowly body to conform with his glorified body by the power that enables him also to bring all things into subjection to himself.

[1]Therefore, my brothers and sisters, whom I love and long for, my joy and crown, in this way stand firm in the Lord, beloved.

Verse before the Gospel: Matthew 17:5

[5] From the shining cloud the Father's voice is

heard:

This is my beloved Son, hear him.

Gospel: Luke 9:28B-36

[28B]Jesus took Peter, John, and James and went up the mountain to pray. [29]While he was praying his face changed in appearance and his clothing became dazzling white. [30]And behold, two men were conversing with him, Moses and Elijah,[31]who appeared in glory and spoke of his exodus that he was going to accomplish in Jerusalem. [32]Peter and his companions had been overcome by sleep, but becoming fully awake, they saw his glory and the two men standing with him. [33]As they were about to part from him, Peter said to Jesus, "Master, it is good that we are here; let us make three tents, one for you, one for Moses, and one for Elijah." But he did not know what he was saying. [34]While he was still speaking, a cloud came and cast a shadow over them, and they became frightened when they entered the cloud. [35]Then from the cloud came a voice that said, "This is my chosen Son; listen to him." [36]After the voice had spoken, Jesus was found alone. They fell silent and did not at that time tell anyone what they had seen.

Third Sunday of Lent, Year C

First Reading: Exodus 3:1-8A, 13-15

[1]Moses was tending the flock of his father-in-law Jethro, the priest of Midian. Leading the flock across the desert, he came to Horeb, the mountain of God. [2]There an angel of the LORD appeared to Moses in fire flaming out of a bush. As he looked on, he was surprised to see that the bush, though on fire, was not consumed. [3]So Moses decided, "I must go over to look at this remarkable sight, and see why the bush is not burned."

[4]When the LORD saw him coming over to look at it more closely, God called out to him from the bush, "Moses! Moses!" He answered, "Here I am." [5]God said, "Come no nearer! Remove the sandals from your feet, for the place where you stand is holy ground. [6]I am the God of your fathers," he continued, "the God of Abraham, the God of Isaac, the God of Jacob." Moses hid his face, for he was afraid to look at God. [7]But the LORD said, "I have witnessed the affliction of my people in Egypt and have heard their cry of complaint against their slave drivers, so I know well what they are suffering. [8A]Therefore I have come down to rescue them from the hands of the Egyptians and lead them out of that land into a good and spacious land, a land flowing with milk and honey."

[13]Moses said to God, "But when I go to the Israelites and say to them, 'The God of your fathers has sent me to you,' if they ask me, 'What is his name?' what am I to tell them?" [14]God replied, "I am who am." Then he added, "This is what you shall tell the Israelites: I AM sent me to you."

[15]God spoke further to Moses, "Thus shall you say to the Israelites: The LORD, the God of your fathers, the God of Abraham, the God of Isaac, the God of Jacob, has sent me to you.

"This is my name forever;
    thus am I to be remembered through all
        generations."

Responsorial Psalm: Psalms 103: 1-2, 3-4, 6-7, 8, 11.

R. [8a] The Lord is kind and merciful.

[1] Bless the LORD, O my soul;
    and all my being, bless his holy name.
[2] Bless the LORD, O my soul,
    and forget not all his benefits.

R. The Lord is kind and merciful.

[3] He pardons all your iniquities,
    heals all your ills,
[4] He redeems your life from destruction,
    crowns you with kindness and
        compassion.

R. The Lord is kind and merciful.

[6] The LORD secures justice
    and the rights of all the oppressed.

^{7} He has made known his ways to Moses,
and his deeds to the children of Israel.
R. The Lord is kind and merciful.
^{8} Merciful and gracious is the LORD,
slow to anger and abounding in kindness.
^{11} For as the heavens are high above the earth,
so surpassing is his kindness toward
those who fear him.
R. The Lord is kind and merciful.

Second Reading: 1 Corinthians 10:1-6, 10-12

^{1}I do not want you to be unaware, brothers and sisters, that our ancestors were all under the cloud and all passed through the sea, ^{2}and all of them were baptized into Moses in the cloud and in the sea. ^{3}All ate the same spiritual food, ^{4}and all drank the same spiritual drink, for they drank from a spiritual rock that followed them, and the rock was the Christ. ^{5}Yet God was not pleased with most of them, for they were struck down in the desert.

^{6}These things happened as examples for us, so that we might not desire evil things, as they did. ^{10}Do not grumble as some of them did, and suffered death by the destroyer. ^{11}These things happened to them as an example, and they have been written down as a warning to us, upon whom the end of the ages has come. ^{12}Therefore, whoever thinks he is standing secure should take care not to fall.

Verse before the Gospel: Matthew 4:17

^{17}Repent, says the Lord;
the kingdom of heaven is at hand.

Gospel: Luke 13:1-9

^{1}Some people told Jesus about the Galileans whose blood Pilate had mingled with the blood of their sacrifices. ^{2}Jesus said to them in reply, "Do you think that because these Galileans suffered in this way they were greater sinners than all other Galileans? ^{3}By no means! But I tell you, if you do not repent, you will all perish as they did! ^{4}Or those eighteen people who were killed when the tower at Siloam fell on them— do you think they were more guilty than everyone else who lived in Jerusalem? ^{5}By no means! But I tell you, if you do not repent, you will all perish as they did!"

^{6}And he told them this parable: "There once was a person who had a fig tree planted in his orchard, and when he came in search of fruit on it but found none, ^{7}he said to the gardener, 'For three years now I have come in search of fruit on this fig tree but have found none. So cut it down. Why should it exhaust the soil?' ^{8}He said to him in reply, 'Sir, leave it for this year also, and I shall cultivate the ground around it and fertilize it; ^{9}it may bear fruit in the future. If not you can cut it down.'"

Fourth Sunday of Lent, Year C
First Reading: Joshua 5:9A, 10-12

[9]The LORD said to Joshua, "Today I have removed the reproach of Egypt from you."

[10]While the Israelites were encamped at Gilgal on the plains of Jericho, they celebrated the Passover on the evening of the fourteenth of the month. [11]On the day after the Passover, they ate of the produce of the land in the form of unleavened cakes and parched grain. On that same day [12]after the Passover, on which they ate of the produce of the land, the manna ceased. No longer was there manna for the Israelites, who that year ate of the yield of the land of Canaan.

Responsorial Psalm: Psalms 34:2-3, 4-5, 6-7.

R. [9a] *Taste and see the goodness of the Lord.*

[2] I will bless the LORD at all times;
    his praise shall be ever in my mouth.
[3] Let my soul glory in the LORD;
    the lowly will hear me and be glad.

R. Taste and see the goodness of the Lord.

[4] Glorify the LORD with me,
    let us together extol his name.
[5] I sought the LORD, and he answered me
    and delivered me from all my fears.

R. Taste and see the goodness of the Lord.

[6] Look to him that you may be radiant with
        joy,
    and your faces may not blush with
        shame.
[7] When the poor one called out, the LORD
        heard,
    and from all his distress he saved him.

R. Taste and see the goodness of the Lord.

Second Reading: 2 Corinthians 5:17-21

[17]Brothers and sisters: Whoever is in Christ is a new creation: the old things have passed away; behold, new things have come. [18]And all this is from God, who has reconciled us to himself through Christ and given us the ministry of reconciliation, [19]namely, God was reconciling the world to himself in Christ, not counting their trespasses against them and entrusting to us the message of reconciliation. [20]So we are ambassadors for Christ, as if God were appealing through us. We implore you on behalf of Christ, be reconciled to God. [21]For our sake he made him be sin who did not know sin, so that we might become the righteousness of God in him.

Verse Before the Gospel: Luke 15:18

¹⁸ I will get up and go to my Father and shall
    say to him:
Father, I have sinned against heaven and
    against you.

Gospel: Luke 15:1-3, 11-32

¹ Tax collectors and sinners were all drawing near to listen to Jesus, ²but the Pharisees and scribes began to complain, saying, "This man welcomes sinners and eats with them." ³So to them, Jesus addressed this parable: ¹¹"A man had two sons, ¹²and the younger son said to his father, 'Father give me the share of your estate that should come to me.' So the father divided the property between them. ¹³After a few days, the younger son collected all his belongings and set off to a distant country where he squandered his inheritance on a life of dissipation. ¹⁴When he had freely spent everything, a severe famine struck that country, and he found himself in dire need. ¹⁵So he hired himself out to one of the local citizens who sent him to his farm to tend the swine. ¹⁶And he longed to eat his fill of the pods on which the swine fed, but nobody gave him any. ¹⁷Coming to his senses he thought, 'How many of my father's hired workers have more than enough food to eat, but here am I, dying from hunger. ¹⁸I shall get up and go to my father and I shall say to him, "Father, I have sinned against heaven and against you. ¹⁹I no longer deserve to be called your son; treat me as you would treat one of your hired workers."' ²⁰So he got up and went back to his father. While he was still a long way off, his father caught sight of him and was filled with compassion. He ran to his son, embraced him and kissed him. ²¹His son said to him, 'Father, I have sinned against heaven and against you; I no longer deserve to be called your son.' ²²But his father ordered his servants, 'Quickly bring the finest robe and put it on him; put a ring on his finger and sandals on his feet. ²³Take the fattened calf and slaughter it. Then let us celebrate with a feast, ²⁴because this son of mine was dead and has come to life again; he was lost, and has been found.' Then the celebration began. ²⁵Now the older son had been out in the field and, on his way back, as he neared the house, he heard the sound of music and dancing. ²⁶He called one of the servants and asked what this might mean. ²⁷The servant said to him, 'Your brother has returned and your father has slaughtered the fattened calf because he has him back safe and sound.' ²⁸He became angry, and when he refused to enter the house, his father came out and pleaded with him. ²⁹He said to his father in reply, 'Look, all these years I served you and not once did I disobey your orders; yet you never gave me even a young goat to feast on with my friends. ³⁰But when your son returns who swallowed up your property with prostitutes, for him, you slaughter the fattened calf.' ³¹He said to him, 'My son, you are here with me always; everything I have is yours. ³²But now we must celebrate and rejoice, because your brother was dead and has come to life again; he was lost and has been found.'"

APRIL 2025

Sunday April 6, 2025

Fifth Sunday of Lent, Year C

First Reading: Isaiah 43:16-21

[16] Thus says the LORD,
 who opens a way in the sea
 and a path in the mighty waters,
[17] who leads out chariots and horsemen,
 a powerful army,
till they lie prostrate together, never to rise,
 snuffed out and quenched like a wick.
[18] Remember not the events of the past,
 the things of long ago consider not;
[19] see, I am doing something new!
 Now it springs forth, do you not perceive
 it?
In the desert I make a way,
 in the wasteland, rivers.
[20] Wild beasts honor me,
 jackals and ostriches,
for I put water in the desert
 and rivers in the wasteland
 for my chosen people to drink,
[21] the people whom I formed for myself,
 that they might announce my praise.

Responsorial Psalm: Psalms 126:1-2, 2-3, 4-5, 6.

R. [3] The Lord has done great things for us; we are filled with joy.

[1] When the LORD brought back the captives of
 Zion,
 we were like men dreaming.
[2AB] Then our mouth was filled with laughter,
 and our tongue with rejoicing.

R. The Lord has done great things for us; we are filled with joy.

[2CD] Then they said among the nations,
 "The LORD has done great things for
 them."
[3] The LORD has done great things for us;
 we are glad indeed.

R. The Lord has done great things for us; we are filled with joy.

[4] Restore our fortunes, O LORD,
 like the torrents in the southern desert.
[5] Those that sow in tears
 shall reap rejoicing.

R. The Lord has done great things for us; we are

filled with joy.
[6] Although they go forth weeping,
carrying the seed to be sown,
They shall come back rejoicing,
carrying their sheaves.
R. The Lord has done great things for us; we are
filled with joy.

Second Reading: Philippians 3:8-14

Brothers and sisters: [8]I consider everything as a loss because of the supreme good of knowing Christ Jesus my Lord. For his sake I have accepted the loss of all things and I consider them so much rubbish, that I may gain Christ [9]and be found in him, not having any righteousness of my own based on the law but that which comes through faith in Christ, the righteousness from God, depending on faith [10] to know him and the power of his resurrection and the sharing of his sufferings by being conformed to his death, [11]if somehow I may attain the resurrection from the dead.

[12]It is not that I have already taken hold of it or have already attained perfect maturity, but I continue my pursuit in hope that I may possess it, since I have indeed been taken possession of by Christ Jesus. [13]Brothers and sisters, I for my part do not consider myself to have taken possession. Just one thing: forgetting what lies behind but straining forward to what lies ahead, [14]I continue my pursuit toward the goal, the prize of God's upward calling, in Christ Jesus.

Verse Before the Gospel: Joel 2:12-13

[12] Even now, says the Lord,
return to me with your whole heart;
[13] for I am gracious and merciful.

Gospel: John 8:1-11

[1]Jesus went to the Mount of Olives. [2]But early in the morning he arrived again in the temple area, and all the people started coming to him, and he sat down and taught them. [3]Then the scribes and the Pharisees brought a woman who had been caught in adultery and made her stand in the middle. [4]They said to him, "Teacher, this woman was caught in the very act of committing adultery. [5]Now in the law, Moses commanded us to stone such women. So what do you say?" [6]They said this to test him, so that they could have some charge to bring against him. Jesus bent down and began to write on the ground with his finger. [7]But when they continued asking him, he straightened up and said to them, "Let the one among you who is without sin be the first to throw a stone at her." [8]Again he bent down and wrote on the ground. [9]And in response, they went away one by one, beginning with the elders. So he was left alone with the woman before him. [10]Then Jesus straightened up and said to her, "Woman, where are they? Has no one condemned

you?" [11]She replied, "No one, sir." Then Jesus said, "Neither do I condemn you. Go, and from now on do not sin any more."

Palm Sunday, Year C
At The Procession with Palms – Gospel – Luke 19:28-40

[28] Jesus proceeded on his journey up to Jerusalem. [29]As he drew near to Bethphage and Bethany at the place called the Mount of Olives, he sent two of his disciples. [30]He said, "Go into the village opposite you, and as you enter it you will find a colt tethered on which no one has ever sat. Untie it and bring it here. [31]And if anyone should ask you, 'Why are you untying it?' you will answer, 'The Master has need of it.'" [32]So those who had been sent went off and found everything just as he had told them. [33]And as they were untying the colt, its owners said to them, "Why are you untying this colt?" [34]They answered, "The Master has need of it." [35]So they brought it to Jesus, threw their cloaks over the colt, and helped Jesus to mount. [36]As he rode along, the people were spreading their cloaks on the road; [37]and now as he was approaching the slope of the Mount of Olives, the whole multitude of his disciples began to praise God aloud with joy for all the mighty deeds they had seen. [38]They proclaimed:

"Blessed is the king who comes
    in the name of the Lord.
Peace in heaven
    and glory in the highest."

[39]Some of the Pharisees in the crowd said to him, "Teacher, rebuke your disciples." [31]He said in reply, "I tell you, if they keep silent, the stones will cry out!"

At The Mass – First Reading - Isaiah 50:4-7

[4] The Lord GOD has given me
    a well-trained tongue,
that I might know how to speak to the weary
    a word that will rouse them.
Morning after morning
    he opens my ear that I may hear;
[5] and I have not rebelled,
    have not turned back.
        [6]I gave my back to those who beat me,
        my cheeks to those who plucked my
            beard;
my face I did not shield
    from buffets and spitting.

[7]The Lord GOD is my help,
    therefore I am not disgraced;

I have set my face like flint,
    knowing that I shall not be put to shame.

Responsorial Psalm: Psalms 22:8-9, 17-18, 19-20, 23-24

R. [2a] *My God, my God, why have you*
              abandoned me?

[8]All who see me scoff at me;
    they mock me with parted lips, they wag
        their heads:
[9] "He relied on the LORD; let him deliver him,
    let him rescue him, if he loves him."

R. *My God, my God, why have you abandoned*
        me?

[17]Indeed, many dogs surround me,
    a pack of evildoers closes in upon me;
[18]They have pierced my hands and my feet;
    I can count all my bones.

R. *My God, my God, why have you abandoned*
        me?

[19]They divide my garments among them,
    and for my vesture they cast lots.
[20]But you, O LORD, be not far from me;
    O my help, hasten to aid me.

R. *My God, my God, why have you abandoned*
        me?

[23]I will proclaim your name to my brethren;
    in the midst of the assembly I will praise
        you:
[24]"You who fear the LORD, praise him;
    all you descendants of Jacob, give glory to
        him;
    revere him, all you descendants of
        Israel!"

R. *My God, my God, why have you abandoned*
        me?

Second Reading: Philippians 2:6-11

[6]Christ Jesus, though he was in the form of
        God,
    did not regard equality with God
    something to be grasped.
[7]Rather, he emptied himself,
    taking the form of a slave,
    coming in human likeness;

and found human in appearance,
[8]he humbled himself,
becoming obedient to the point of death,
even death on a cross.
[9]Because of this, God greatly exalted him
and bestowed on him the name
which is above every name,
[10]that at the name of Jesus
every knee should bend,
of those in heaven and on earth and
under the earth,
[11]and every tongue confess that
Jesus Christ is Lord,
to the glory of God the Father.

Verse Before the Gospel: Philippians 2:8-9

[8]Christ became obedient to the point of death,
even death on a cross.
[9]Because of this, God greatly exalted him
and bestowed on him the name which is
above every name.

Gospel: Luke 22:14-23:56

[14]When the hour came, Jesus took his place at table with the apostles. [15]He said to them, "I have eagerly desired to eat this Passover with you before I suffer, [16]for, I tell you, I shall not eat it again until there is fulfillment in the kingdom of God." [17]Then he took a cup, gave thanks, and said, "Take this and share it among yourselves; [18]for I tell you that from this time on I shall not drink of the fruit of the vine until the kingdom of God comes." [19]Then he took the bread, said the blessing, broke it, and gave it to them, saying, "This is my body, which will be given for you; do this in memory of me." [20]And likewise the cup after they had eaten, saying, "This cup is the new covenant in my blood, which will be shed for you.

[21]"And yet behold, the hand of the one who is to betray me is with me on the table; [22]for the Son of Man indeed goes as it has been determined; but woe to that man by whom he is betrayed." [23]And they began to debate among themselves who among them would do such a deed.

[24]Then an argument broke out among them about which of them should be regarded as the greatest. [25]He said to them, "The kings of the Gentiles lord it over them and those in authority over them are addressed as 'Benefactors'; [26]but among you it shall not be so. Rather, let the greatest among you be as the youngest, and the leader as the servant. [27]For who is greater: the one seated at table or the one who serves? Is it not the one seated at table? I am among you as the one who serves. [28]It is you who have stood by me in my trials; [29]and I confer a kingdom on you, just as my Father has conferred one on me, [30]that you may eat

and drink at my table in my kingdom; and you will sit on thrones judging the twelve tribes of Israel.

[31]"Simon, Simon, behold Satan has demanded to sift all of you like wheat, [32]but I have prayed that your own faith may not fail; and once you have turned back, you must strengthen your brothers." [33]He said to him, "Lord, I am prepared to go to prison and to die with you." [34]But he replied, "I tell you, Peter, before the cock crows this day, you will deny three times that you know me."

[35]He said to them, "When I sent you forth without a money bag or a sack or sandals, were you in need of anything?" "No, nothing, " they replied. [36]He said to them, "But now one who has a money bag should take it, and likewise a sack, and one who does not have a sword should sell his cloak and buy one. [37]For I tell you that this Scripture must be fulfilled in me, namely, *He was counted among the wicked*; and indeed what is written about me is coming to fulfillment." [38]Then they said, "Lord, look, there are two swords here." But he replied, "It is enough!"

[39]Then going out, he went, as was his custom, to the Mount of Olives, and the disciples followed him. [40]When he arrived at the place he said to them, "Pray that you may not undergo the test." [41]After withdrawing about a stone's throw from them and kneeling, he prayed, [42]saying, "Father, if you are willing, take this cup away from me; still, not my will but yours be done." [43]And to strengthen him an angel from heaven appeared to him. [44]He was in such agony and he prayed so fervently that his sweat became like drops of blood falling on the ground. [45]When he rose from prayer and returned to his disciples, he found them sleeping from grief. [46]He said to them, "Why are you sleeping? Get up and pray that you may not undergo the test."

[47]While he was still speaking, a crowd approached and in front was one of the Twelve, a man named Judas. He went up to Jesus to kiss him. [48]Jesus said to him, "Judas, are you betraying the Son of Man with a kiss?" [49]His disciples realized what was about to happen, and they asked, "Lord, shall we strike with a sword?" [50]And one of them struck the high priest's servant and cut off his right ear. [51]But Jesus said in reply, "Stop, no more of this!" Then he touched the servant's ear and healed him. [52]And Jesus said to the chief priests and temple guards and elders who had come for him, "Have you come out as against a robber, with swords and clubs? [53]Day after day I was with you in the temple area, and you did not seize me; but this is your hour, the time for the power of darkness."

[54]After arresting him they led him away and took him into the house of the high priest; Peter was following at a distance. [55]They lit a fire in the middle of the courtyard and sat around it, and Peter sat down with them. [56]When a maid saw him seated in the light, she looked intently at him and said, "This man too was with him." [57]But he denied it saying, "Woman, I do not know him." [58]A short while later someone else saw him and said, "You too are one of them"; but Peter answered, "My friend, I am not." [59]About an hour later, still another insisted, "Assuredly, this man too was with him, for he also is a Galilean." [60]But Peter said, "My friend, I do not know what you are talking about." Just as he was saying this, the cock crowed, [61]and the Lord turned and looked at Peter; and Peter remembered the word of the Lord, how he had said to him, "Before the cock crows today, you will deny me

three times." [62]He went out and began to weep bitterly. [63]The men who held Jesus in custody were ridiculing and beating him. [64]They blindfolded him and questioned him, saying, "Prophesy! Who is it that struck you?" [65]And they reviled him in saying many other things against him.

[66]When day came the council of elders of the people met, both chief priests and scribes, and they brought him before their Sanhedrin. [67]They said, "If you are the Christ, tell us," but he replied to them, "If I tell you, you will not believe, [68]and if I question, you will not respond. [69]But from this time on the Son of Man will be seated at the right hand of the power of God." [70]They all asked, "Are you then the Son of God?" He replied to them, "You say that I am." [71]Then they said, "What further need have we for testimony? We have heard it from his own mouth."

[1]Then the whole assembly of them arose and brought him before Pilate. [2]They brought charges against him, saying, "We found this man misleading our people; he opposes the payment of taxes to Caesar and maintains that he is the Christ, a king." [3] Pilate asked him, "Are you the king of the Jews?" He said to him in reply, "You say so." [4] Pilate then addressed the chief priests and the crowds, "I find this man not guilty." [5] But they were adamant and said, "He is inciting the people with his teaching throughout all Judea, from Galilee where he began even to here."

[6]On hearing this Pilate asked if the man was a Galilean; [7]and upon learning that he was under Herod's jurisdiction, he sent him to Herod who was in Jerusalem at that time. [8]Herod was very glad to see Jesus; he had been wanting to see him for a long time, for he had heard about him and had been hoping to see him perform some sign. [9]He questioned him at length, but he gave him no answer. [10]The chief priests and scribes, meanwhile, stood by accusing him harshly. [11]Herod and his soldiers treated him contemptuously and mocked him, and after clothing him in resplendent garb, he sent him back to Pilate. [12]Herod and Pilate became friends that very day, even though they had been enemies formerly. [13]Pilate then summoned the chief priests, the rulers, and the people [14]and said to them, "You brought this man to me and accused him of inciting the people to revolt. I have conducted my investigation in your presence and have not found this man guilty of the charges you have brought against him, [15]nor did Herod, for he sent him back to us. So no capital crime has been committed by him. [16]Therefore I shall have him flogged and then release him."

[18] But all together they shouted out, "Away with this man! Release Barabbas to us." [19]—Now Barabbas had been imprisoned for a rebellion that had taken place in the city and for murder.— [20]Again Pilate addressed them, still wishing to release Jesus, [21]but they continued their shouting, "Crucify him! Crucify him!" [22] Pilate addressed them a third time, "What evil has this man done? I found him guilty of no capital crime. Therefore I shall have him flogged and then release him." [23]With loud shouts, however, they persisted in calling for his crucifixion, and their voices prevailed. [24] The verdict of Pilate was that their demand should be granted. [25]So he released the man who had been imprisoned for rebellion and murder, for whom they asked, and he handed Jesus over to them to deal with as they wished.

[26]As they led him away they took hold of a certain Simon, a Cyrenian, who was coming in from the country; and after laying the cross on him, they made him

carry it behind Jesus. [27] A large crowd of people followed Jesus, including many women who mourned and lamented him. [28] Jesus turned to them and said, "Daughters of Jerusalem, do not weep for me; weep instead for yourselves and for your children [29]for indeed, the days are coming when people will say, 'Blessed are the barren, the wombs that never bore and the breasts that never nursed.' [30]At that time people will say to the mountains, 'Fall upon us!' and to the hills, 'Cover us!' [31]for if these things are done when the wood is green what will happen when it is dry?" [32]Now two others, both criminals, were led away with him to be executed.

[33]When they came to the place called the Skull, they crucified him and the criminals there, one on his right, the other on his left. [34]Then Jesus said, "Father, forgive them, they know not what they do." They divided his garments by casting lots. [35]The people stood by and watched; the rulers, meanwhile, sneered at him and said, "He saved others, let him save himself if he is the chosen one, the Christ of God." [36]Even the soldiers jeered at him. As they approached to offer him wine [37]they called out, "If you are King of the Jews, save yourself." [38]Above him there was an inscription that read, "This is the King of the Jews."

[39]Now one of the criminals hanging there reviled Jesus, saying, "Are you not the Christ? Save yourself and us." [40]The other, however, rebuking him, said in reply, "Have you no fear of God, for you are subject to the same condemnation? [41]And indeed, we have been condemned justly, for the sentence we received corresponds to our crimes, but this man has done nothing criminal." [42]Then he said, "Jesus, remember me when you come into your kingdom." [43]He replied to him, "Amen, I say to you, today you will be with me in Paradise."

[44]It was now about noon and darkness came over the whole land until three in the afternoon [45]because of an eclipse of the sun. Then the veil of the temple was torn down the middle. [46]Jesus cried out in a loud voice, "Father, into your hands I commend my spirit"; and when he had said this he breathed his last.

(Here all kneel and pause for a short time)

[47]The centurion who witnessed what had happened glorified God and said, "This man was innocent beyond doubt." [48]When all the people who had gathered for this spectacle saw what had happened, they returned home beating their breasts; [49]but all his acquaintances stood at a distance, including the women who had followed him from Galilee and saw these events.

[50]Now there was a virtuous and righteous man named Joseph who, though he was a member of the council, [51]had not consented to their plan of action. He came from the Jewish town of Arimathea and was awaiting the kingdom of God. [52]He went to Pilate and asked for the body of Jesus. [53]After he had taken the body down, he wrapped it in a linen cloth and laid him in a rock-hewn tomb in which no one had yet been buried. [54]It was the day of preparation, and the Sabbath was about to begin. [55]The women who had come from Galilee with him followed behind, and when they had seen the tomb and the way in which his body was laid in it, [56]they returned and prepared spices and perfumed oils. Then they rested on the Sabbath according to the commandment.

Or Luke 23:1-49

[1]The elders of the people, chief priests and scribes, arose and brought him before Pilate. [2] They brought charges against him, saying, "We found this man misleading our people; he opposes the payment of taxes to Caesar and maintains that he is the Christ, a king." [3] Pilate asked him, "Are you the king of the Jews?" He said to him in reply, "You say so." [4] Pilate then addressed the chief priests and the crowds, "I find this man not guilty." [5] But they were adamant and said, "He is inciting the people with his teaching throughout all Judea, from Galilee where he began even to here."

[6]On hearing this Pilate asked if the man was a Galilean; [7]and upon learning that he was under Herod's jurisdiction, he sent him to Herod who was in Jerusalem at that time. [8]Herod was very glad to see Jesus; he had been wanting to see him for a long time, for he had heard about him and had been hoping to see him perform some sign. [9]He questioned him at length, but he gave him no answer. [10]The chief priests and scribes, meanwhile, stood by accusing him harshly. [11]Herod and his soldiers treated him contemptuously and mocked him, and after clothing him in resplendent garb, he sent him back to Pilate. [12]Herod and Pilate became friends that very day, even though they had been enemies formerly. [13]Pilate then summoned the chief priests, the rulers, and the people [14]and said to them, "You brought this man to me and accused him of inciting the people to revolt. I have conducted my investigation in your presence and have not found this man guilty of the charges you have brought against him, [15]nor did Herod, for he sent him back to us. So no capital crime has been committed by him. [16]Therefore I shall have him flogged and then release him."

[18]But all together they shouted out, "Away with this man! Release Barabbas to us." [19]—Now Barabbas had been imprisoned for a rebellion that had taken place in the city and for murder.— [20]Again Pilate addressed them, still wishing to release Jesus, [21]but they continued their shouting, "Crucify him! Crucify him!" [22]Pilate addressed them a third time, "What evil has this man done? I found him guilty of no capital crime. Therefore I shall have him flogged and then release him." [23]With loud shouts, however, they persisted in calling for his crucifixion, and their voices prevailed. [24]The verdict of Pilate was that their demand should be granted. [25]So he released the man who had been imprisoned for rebellion and murder, for whom they asked, and he handed Jesus over to them to deal with as they wished.

[26]As they led him away they took hold of a certain Simon, a Cyrenian, who was coming in from the country; and after laying the cross on him, they made him carry it behind Jesus. [27]A large crowd of people followed Jesus, including many women who mourned and lamented him. [28]Jesus turned to them and said, "Daughters of Jerusalem, do not weep for me; weep instead for yourselves and for your children [29]for indeed, the days are coming when people will say, 'Blessed are the barren, the wombs that never bore and the breasts that never nursed.' [30]At that time people will say to the mountains, 'Fall upon us!' and to the hills, 'Cover us!' [31]for if these things are done when the wood is green what will happen when it is dry?" [32]Now two others, both criminals, were led away with him to be executed.

[33]When they came to the place called the Skull, they crucified him and the criminals there, one on his right, the other on his left. [34]Then Jesus said, "Father,

forgive them, they know not what they do." They divided his garments by casting lots. [35]The people stood by and watched; the rulers, meanwhile, sneered at him and said, "He saved others, let him save himself if he is the chosen one, the Christ of God." [36]Even the soldiers jeered at him. As they approached to offer him wine [37]they called out, "If you are King of the Jews, save yourself." [38]Above him there was an inscription that read, "This is the King of the Jews."

[39]Now one of the criminals hanging there reviled Jesus, saying, "Are you not the Christ? Save yourself and us." [40]The other, however, rebuking him, said in reply, "Have you no fear of God, for you are subject to the same condemnation? [41]And indeed, we have been condemned justly, for the sentence we received corresponds to our crimes, but this man has done nothing criminal." [42]Then he said, "Jesus, remember me when you come into your kingdom." [43]He replied to him, "Amen, I say to you, today you will be with me in Paradise." [44]It was now about noon and darkness came over the whole land until three in the afternoon [45]because of an eclipse of the sun. Then the veil of the temple was torn down the middle. [46]Jesus cried out in a loud voice, "Father, into your hands I commend my spirit"; and when he had said this he breathed his last.

(Here all kneel and pause for a short time)

[47]The centurion who witnessed what had happened glorified God and said, "This man was innocent beyond doubt." [48]When all the people who had gathered for this spectacle saw what had happened, they returned home beating their breasts; [49]but all his acquaintances stood at a distance, including the women who had followed him from Galilee and saw these events.

Sunday April 20, 2025
Easter Sunday

First Reading: Acts 10:34A, 37-43

[34A] Peter proceeded to speak and said: [37] "You know what has happened all over Judea, beginning in Galilee after the baptism that John preached, [38] how God anointed Jesus of Nazareth with the Holy Spirit and power. He went about doing good and healing all those oppressed by the devil, for God was with him. [39] We are witnesses of all that he did both in the country of the Jews and in Jerusalem. They put him to death by hanging him on a tree. [40] This man God raised on the third day and granted that he be visible, [41] not to all the people, but to us, the witnesses chosen by God in advance, who ate and drank with him after he rose from the dead. [42] He commissioned us to preach to the people and testify that he is the one appointed by God as judge of the living and the dead. [43] To him all the prophets bear witness, that everyone who believes in him will receive forgiveness of sins through his name."

Responsorial Psalm: Psalms 118:1-2, 16-17, 22-23.

R. [24] *This is the day the Lord has made; let us*
rejoice and be glad. or: R. *Alleluia.*

[1] Give thanks to the LORD, for he is good,
for his mercy endures forever.

² Let the house of Israel say,
     "His mercy endures forever."
**R. This is the day the Lord has made; let us
          rejoice and be glad.** or: **R. Alleluia.**
¹⁶ The right hand of the LORD has struck with
          power;
     the right hand of the LORD is exalted.
¹⁷ I shall not die, but live,
     and declare the works of the LORD.
**R. This is the day the Lord has made; let us
          rejoice and be glad.** or: **R. Alleluia.**
²² The stone which the builders rejected
     has become the cornerstone.
²³ By the LORD has this been done;
     it is wonderful in our eyes.
**R. This is the day the Lord has made; let us
          rejoice and be glad.** or: **R. Alleluia.**

Second Reading: Colossians 3:1-4

Brothers and sisters: ¹ If then you were raised with Christ, seek what is above, where Christ is seated at the right hand of God. ² Think of what is above, not of what is on earth. ³ For you have died, and your life is hidden with Christ in God. ⁴ When Christ your life appears, then you too will appear with him in glory.

Or 1 Corinthians 5:6B-8

Brothers and sisters: ^{6B} Do you not know that a little yeast leavens all the dough? ⁷ Clear out the old yeast, so that you may become a fresh batch of dough, inasmuch as you are unleavened. For our paschal lamb, Christ, has been sacrificed. ⁸ Therefore, let us celebrate the feast, not with the old yeast, the yeast of malice and wickedness, but with the unleavened bread of sincerity and truth.

Sequence - *Victimae Paschali Laudes*

Christians, to the Paschal Victim
Offer your thankful praises!
A Lamb the sheep redeems;
Christ, who only is sinless,
Reconciles sinners to the Father.
Death and life have contended in that combat stupendous:
The Prince of life, who died, reigns immortal.
Speak, Mary, declaring
What you saw, wayfaring.
"The tomb of Christ, who is living,
The glory of Jesus' resurrection;
Bright angels attesting,

The shroud and napkin resting.
Yes, Christ my hope is arisen;
To Galilee he goes before you."
Christ indeed from death is risen, our new life obtaining.
Have mercy, victor King, ever reigning!
Amen. Alleluia.

Alleluia: cf. 1 Corinthians 5:7B-8A
R. Alleluia, alleluia.
[7B] Christ, our paschal lamb, has been
sacrificed;
[8A] let us then feast with joy in the Lord.
R. Alleluia, alleluia.

Gospel: John 20:1-9
[1] On the first day of the week, Mary of Magdala came to the tomb early in the morning, while it was still dark, and saw the stone removed from the tomb. [2] So she ran and went to Simon Peter and to the other disciple whom Jesus loved, and told them, "They have taken the Lord from the tomb, and we don't know where they put him." [3] So Peter and the other disciple went out and came to the tomb. [4] They both ran, but the other disciple ran faster than Peter and arrived at the tomb first; [5] he bent down and saw the burial cloths there, but did not go in. [6] When Simon Peter arrived after him, he went into the tomb and saw the burial cloths there, [7] and the cloth that had covered his head, not with the burial cloths but rolled up in a separate place. [8] Then the other disciple also went in, the one who had arrived at the tomb first, and he saw and believed. [9] For they did not yet understand the Scripture that he had to rise from the dead.

Or Luke 24:1-12
[1] At daybreak on the first day of the week the women who had come from Galilee with Jesus took the spices they had prepared and went to the tomb. [2] They found the stone rolled away from the tomb; [3] but when they entered, they did not find the body of the Lord Jesus. [4] While they were puzzling over this, behold, two men in dazzling garments appeared to them. [5] They were terrified and bowed their faces to the ground. They said to them, "Why do you seek the living one among the dead? [6] He is not here, but he has been raised. Remember what he said to you while he was still in Galilee, [7] that the Son of Man must be handed over to sinners and be crucified, and rise on the third day." [8] And they remembered his words. [9] Then they returned from the tomb and announced all these things to the eleven and to all the others. [10] The women were Mary Magdalene, Joanna, and Mary the mother of James; the others who accompanied them also told this to the apostles, [11] but their story seemed like nonsense and they did not believe them. [12] But Peter got up and ran to the tomb, bent down, and saw the burial cloths alone; then he went home amazed at what had happened.

Or Luke: 24:13-35
At an afternoon or evening Mass.

¹³ That very day, the first day of the week, two of Jesus' disciples were going to a village seven miles from Jerusalem called Emmaus, ¹⁴ and they were conversing about all the things that had occurred. ¹⁵ And it happened that while they were conversing and debating, Jesus himself drew near and walked with them, ¹⁶ but their eyes were prevented from recognizing him. ¹⁷ He asked them, "What are you discussing as you walk along?" They stopped, looking downcast. ¹⁸ One of them, named Cleopas, said to him in reply, "Are you the only visitor to Jerusalem who does not know of the things that have taken place there in these days?" ¹⁹ And he replied to them, "What sort of things?" They said to him, "The things that happened to Jesus the Nazarene, who was a prophet mighty in deed and word before God and all the people, ²⁰ how our chief priests and rulers both handed him over to a sentence of death and crucified him. ²¹ But we were hoping that he would be the one to redeem Israel; and besides all this, it is now the third day since this took place. ²² Some women from our group, however, have astounded us: they were at the tomb early in the morning ²³ and did not find his body; they came back and reported that they had indeed seen a vision of angels who announced that he was alive. ²⁴ Then some of those with us went to the tomb and found things just as the women had described, but him they did not see." ²⁵ And he said to them, "Oh, how foolish you are! How slow of heart to believe all that the prophets spoke! ²⁶ Was it not necessary that the Christ should suffer these things and enter into his glory?" ²⁷ Then beginning with Moses and all the prophets, he interpreted to them what referred to him in all the Scriptures. ²⁸ As they approached the village to which they were going, he gave the impression that he was going on farther. ²⁹ But they urged him, "Stay with us, for it is nearly evening and the day is almost over." So he went in to stay with them. ³⁰ And it happened that, while he was with them at table, he took bread, said the blessing, broke it, and gave it to them. ³¹ With that their eyes were opened and they recognized him, but he vanished from their sight.

³² Then they said to each other, "Were not our hearts burning within us while he spoke to us on the way and opened the Scriptures to us?" ³³ So they set out at once and returned to Jerusalem where they found gathered together the eleven and those with them ³⁴ who were saying, "The Lord has truly been raised and has appeared to Simon!" ³⁵ Then the two recounted what had taken place on the way and how he was made known to them in the breaking of bread.

Sunday April 27, 2025
Second Sunday of Easter – Divine Mercy Sunday Year C
First Reading: Acts 5:12-16

¹²Many signs and wonders were done among the people at the hands of the apostles. They were all together in Solomon's portico. ¹³None of the others dared to join them, but the people esteemed them. ¹⁴Yet more than ever, believers in the Lord, great numbers of men and women, were added to them. ¹⁵Thus they even carried the sick out into the streets and laid them on cots and mats so that when

Peter came by, at least his shadow might fall on one or another of them. [16]A large number of people from the towns in the vicinity of Jerusalem also gathered, bringing the sick and those disturbed by unclean spirits, and they were all cured.

Responsorial Psalm: Psalms 118:2-4, 13-15, 22-24

R. [(1)] *Give thanks to the Lord for he is good,*
         his love is everlasting. or: *R. Alleluia.*

[2] Let the house of Israel say,
     "His mercy endures forever."
[3] Let the house of Aaron say,
     "His mercy endures forever."
[4] Let those who fear the LORD say,
     "His mercy endures forever."

R. *Give thanks to the Lord for he is good, his*
         love is everlasting. or: *R. Alleluia.*

[13] I was hard pressed and was falling,
     but the LORD helped me.
[14] My strength and my courage is the LORD,
     and he has been my savior.
[15] The joyful shout of victory
     in the tents of the just:

R. *Give thanks to the Lord for he is good, his*
         love is everlasting. or: *R. Alleluia.*

[22] The stone which the builders rejected
     has become the cornerstone.
[23] By the LORD has this been done;
     it is wonderful in our eyes.
[24] This is the day the LORD has made;
     let us be glad and rejoice in it.

R. *Give thanks to the Lord for he is good, his*
         love is everlasting. or: *R. Alleluia.*

Second Reading: Revelation 1:9-11A, 12-13, 17-19

[9] I, John, your brother, who share with you the distress, the kingdom, and the endurance we have in Jesus, found myself on the island called Patmos because I proclaimed God's word and gave testimony to Jesus. [10] I was caught up in spirit on the Lord's day and heard behind me a voice as loud as a trumpet, [11A] which said, "Write on a scroll what you see." [12]Then I turned to see whose voice it was that spoke to me, and when I turned, I saw seven gold lampstands [13]and in the midst of the lampstands one like a son of man, wearing an ankle-length robe, with a gold sash around his chest.

     [17]When I caught sight of him, I fell down at his feet as though dead. He touched me with his right hand and said, "Do not be afraid. I am the first and the last, [18]the one who lives. Once I was dead, but now I am alive forever and ever. I

hold the keys to death and the netherworld. [19]Write down, therefore, what you have seen, and what is happening, and what will happen afterwards."

Alleluia: John 20:29
R. Alleluia, alleluia.
[29]You believe in me, Thomas, because you
    have seen me, says the Lord;
Blessed are those who have not seen me, but
    still believe!
R. Alleluia, alleluia.

Gospel: John 20:19-31
[19]On the evening of that first day of the week, when the doors were locked, where the disciples were, for fear of the Jews, Jesus came and stood in their midst and said to them, "Peace be with you." [20]When he had said this, he showed them his hands and his side. The disciples rejoiced when they saw the Lord. [21]Jesus said to them again, "Peace be with you. As the Father has sent me, so I send you." [22]And when he had said this, he breathed on them and said to them, "Receive the Holy Spirit. [23]Whose sins you forgive are forgiven them, and whose sins you retain are retained."

[24]Thomas, called Didymus, one of the Twelve, was not with them when Jesus came. [25]So the other disciples said to him, "We have seen the Lord." But he said to them, "Unless I see the mark of the nails in his hands and put my finger into the nailmarks and put my hand into his side, I will not believe."

[26]Now a week later his disciples were again inside and Thomas was with them. Jesus came, although the doors were locked, and stood in their midst and said, "Peace be with you." [27]Then he said to Thomas, "Put your finger here and see my hands, and bring your hand and put it into my side, and do not be unbelieving, but believe." [28]Thomas answered and said to him, "My Lord and my God!" [29]Jesus said to him, "Have you come to believe because you have seen me? Blessed are those who have not seen and have believed."

[30]Now Jesus did many other signs in the presence of his disciples that are not written in this book. [31]But these are written that you may come to believe that Jesus is the Christ, the Son of God, and that through this belief you may have life in his name.

MAY 2025
Sunday May 4, 2025
Third Sunday of Easter Year C
First Reading: Acts 5:27-32, 40B-41
[27]When the captain and the court officers had brought the apostles in and made them stand before the Sanhedrin, the high priest questioned them, [28]"We gave you strict orders, did we not, to stop teaching in that name? Yet you have filled Jerusalem with your teaching and want to bring this man's blood upon us." [29]But

Peter and the apostles said in reply, "We must obey God rather than men. [30]The God of our ancestors raised Jesus, though you had him killed by hanging him on a tree. [31]God exalted him at his right hand as leader and savior to grant Israel repentance and forgiveness of sins. [32]We are witnesses of these things, as is the Holy Spirit whom God has given to those who obey him."

[40B]The Sanhedrin ordered the apostles to stop speaking in the name of Jesus, and dismissed them. [41]So they left the presence of the Sanhedrin, rejoicing that they had been found worthy to suffer dishonor for the sake of the name.

Responsorial Psalm: Psalms 30:2, 4, 5-6, 11-12, 13

R. [2a] *I will praise you, Lord, for you have rescued me*. or: *R. Alleluia*.

[2] I will extol you, O LORD, for you drew me clear
and did not let my enemies rejoice over me.
[4] O LORD, you brought me up from the netherworld;
you preserved me from among those going down into the pit.

R. *I will praise you, Lord, for you have rescued me*. or: *R. Alleluia*.

[5] Sing praise to the LORD, you his faithful ones,
and give thanks to his holy name.
[6] For his anger lasts but a moment;
a lifetime, his good will.
At nightfall, weeping enters in,
but with the dawn, rejoicing.

R. *I will praise you, Lord, for you have rescued me*. or: *R. Alleluia*.

[11] Hear, O LORD, and have pity on me;
O LORD, be my helper.
[12A] You changed my mourning into dancing;
[13C] O LORD, my God, forever will I give you thanks.

R. *I will praise you, Lord, for you have rescued me*. or: *R. Alleluia*.

Second Reading: Revelation 5:11-14

[11] I, John, looked and heard the voices of many angels who surrounded the throne and the living creatures and the elders. They were countless in number, [12]and they cried out in a loud voice:

"Worthy is the Lamb that was slain

> to receive power and riches, wisdom and
> > strength,
> honor and glory and blessing."

[13]Then I heard every creature in heaven and on earth and under the earth and in the sea, everything in the universe, cry out:

> "To the one who sits on the throne and to the
> > Lamb
> be blessing and honor, glory and might,
> forever and ever."

[14]The four living creatures answered, "Amen," and the elders fell down and worshiped.

Alleluia: Luke 24:32
R. Alleluia, alleluia.
Christ is risen, creator of all;
he has shown pity on all people.
R. Alleluia, alleluia.

Gospel: John 21:1-19
[1]At that time, Jesus revealed himself again to his disciples at the Sea of Tiberias. He revealed himself in this way. [2] Together were Simon Peter, Thomas called Didymus, Nathanael from Cana in Galilee, Zebedee's sons, and two others of his disciples. [3] Simon Peter said to them, "I am going fishing." They said to him, "We also will come with you." So they went out and got into the boat, but that night they caught nothing. [4] When it was already dawn, Jesus was standing on the shore; but the disciples did not realize that it was Jesus. [5]Jesus said to them, "Children, have you caught anything to eat?" They answered him, "No." [6]So he said to them, "Cast the net over the right side of the boat and you will find something." So they cast it, and were not able to pull it in because of the number of fish. [7]So the disciple whom Jesus loved said to Peter, "It is the Lord." When Simon Peter heard that it was the Lord, he tucked in his garment, for he was lightly clad, and jumped into the sea. [8] The other disciples came in the boat, for they were not far from shore, only about a hundred yards, dragging the net with the fish. [9] When they climbed out on shore, they saw a charcoal fire with fish on it and bread. [10]Jesus said to them, "Bring some of the fish you just caught."
[11] So Simon Peter went over and dragged the net ashore full of one hundred fifty-three large fish. Even though there were so many, the net was not torn. [12] Jesus said to them, "Come, have breakfast." And none of the disciples dared to ask him, "Who are you?" because they realized it was the Lord. [13] Jesus came over and took the bread and gave it to them, and in like manner the fish. [14]This was now the third time Jesus was revealed to his disciples after being raised from the dead.

¹⁵When they had finished breakfast, Jesus said to Simon Peter, "Simon, son of John, do you love me more than these?" Simon Peter answered him, "Yes, Lord, you know that I love you." Jesus said to him, "Feed my lambs." ¹⁶He then said to Simon Peter a second time, "Simon, son of John, do you love me?" Simon Peter answered him, "Yes, Lord, you know that I love you." Jesus said to him, "Tend my sheep." ¹⁷Jesus said to him the third time, "Simon, son of John, do you love me?" Peter was distressed that Jesus had said to him a third time, "Do you love me?" and he said to him, "Lord, you know everything; you know that I love you." Jesus said to him, "Feed my sheep. ¹⁸Amen, amen, I say to you, when you were younger, you used to dress yourself and go where you wanted; but when you grow old, you will stretch out your hands, and someone else will dress you and lead you where you do not want to go." ¹⁹He said this signifying by what kind of death he would glorify God. And when he had said this, he said to him, "Follow me."

Or John 21:1-14

¹At that time, Jesus revealed himself again to his disciples at the Sea of Tiberias. He revealed himself in this way. ²Together were Simon Peter, Thomas called Didymus, Nathanael from Cana in Galilee, Zebedee's sons, and two others of his disciples. ³ Simon Peter said to them, "I am going fishing." They said to him, "We also will come with you." So they went out and got into the boat, but that night they caught nothing. ⁴ When it was already dawn, Jesus was standing on the shore; but the disciples did not realize that it was Jesus. ⁵Jesus said to them, "Children, have you caught anything to eat?" They answered him, "No." ⁶ So he said to them, "Cast the net over the right side of the boat and you will find something." So they cast it, and were not able to pull it in because of the number of fish. ⁷ So the disciple whom Jesus loved said to Peter, "It is the Lord." When Simon Peter heard that it was the Lord, he tucked in his garment, for he was lightly clad, and jumped into the sea. ⁸ The other disciples came in the boat, for they were not far from shore, only about a hundred yards, dragging the net with the fish. ⁹When they climbed out on shore, they saw a charcoal fire with fish on it and bread. ¹⁰Jesus said to them, "Bring some of the fish you just caught." ¹¹So Simon Peter went over and dragged the net ashore full of one hundred fifty-three large fish. Even though there were so many, the net was not torn. ¹²Jesus said to them, "Come, have breakfast." And none of the disciples dared to ask him, "Who are you?" because they realized it was the Lord. ¹³Jesus came over and took the bread and gave it to them, and in like manner the fish. ¹⁴This was now the third time Jesus was revealed to his disciples after being raised from the dead.

Sunday May 11, 2025
Fourth Sunday of Easter, Year C
First Reading: Acts 13:14, 43-52

¹⁴Paul and Barnabas continued on from Perga and reached Antioch in Pisidia. On the sabbath they entered the synagogue and took their seats. ⁴³Many Jews and worshipers who were converts to Judaism followed Paul and Barnabas, who spoke to them and urged them to remain faithful to the grace of God.

⁴⁴On the following sabbath almost the whole city gathered to hear the word of the Lord. ⁴⁵When the Jews saw the crowds, they were filled with jealousy and with violent abuse contradicted what Paul said. ⁴⁶Both Paul and Barnabas spoke out boldly and said, "It was necessary that the word of God be spoken to you first, but since you reject it and condemn yourselves as unworthy of eternal life, we now turn to the Gentiles. ⁴⁷For so the Lord has commanded us, *I have made you a light to the Gentiles, that you may be an instrument of salvation to the ends of the earth.*"

⁴⁸The Gentiles were delighted when they heard this and glorified the word of the Lord. All who were destined for eternal life came to believe, ⁴⁹and the word of the Lord continued to spread through the whole region. ⁵⁰The Jews, however, incited the women of prominence who were worshipers and the leading men of the city, stirred up a persecution against Paul and Barnabas, and expelled them from their territory. ⁵¹So they shook the dust from their feet in protest against them, and went to Iconium. ⁵²The disciples were filled with joy and the Holy Spirit.

Responsorial Psalm: Psalms 100:1-2, 3, 5

R. *(3c)* **We are his people, the sheep of his flock**. or: R. **Alleluia**.
¹ Sing joyfully to the LORD, all you lands;
² serve the LORD with gladness;
   come before him with joyful song.
R. **We are his people, the sheep of his flock**. or: R. **Alleluia**.
³ Know that the LORD is God;
   he made us, his we are;
   his people, the flock he tends.
R. **We are his people, the sheep of his flock**. or: R. **Alleluia**.
⁵ The LORD is good:
   his kindness endures forever,
   and his faithfulness, to all generations.
R. **We are his people, the sheep of his flock**. or: R. **Alleluia**.

Second Reading: Revelation 7:9, 14B-17

⁹ I, John, had a vision of a great multitude, which no one could count, from every nation, race, people, and tongue. They stood before the throne and before the Lamb, wearing white robes and holding palm branches in their hands.

¹⁴ᴮThen one of the elders said to me, "These are the ones who have survived the time of great distress; they have washed their robes and made them white in the blood of the Lamb.

¹⁵"For this reason they stand before God's throne and worship him day and night in his temple. The one who sits on the throne will shelter them. ¹⁶They will not hunger or thirst anymore, nor will the sun or any heat strike them. ¹⁷For the Lamb who is in the center of the throne will shepherd them and lead them to springs of life-giving water, and God will wipe away every tear from their eyes."

Alleluia: John 10:14

R. Alleluia, alleluia.
[14] I am the good shepherd, says the Lord;
I know my sheep, and mine know me.
R. Alleluia, alleluia.

Gospel: John 10:27-30

Jesus said: [27]"My sheep hear my voice; I know them, and they follow me. [28]I give them eternal life, and they shall never perish. No one can take them out of my hand. [29]My Father, who has given them to me, is greater than all, and no one can take them out of the Father's hand. [30]The Father and I are one."

Sunday May 18, 2025
Fifth Sunday of Easter, Year C
First Reading: Acts 14:21-27

[21] After Paul and Barnabas had proclaimed the good news to that city and made a considerable number of disciples, they returned to Lystra and to Iconium and to Antioch. [22]They strengthened the spirits of the disciples and exhorted them to persevere in the faith, saying, "It is necessary for us to undergo many hardships to enter the kingdom of God." [23]They appointed elders for them in each church and, with prayer and fasting, commended them to the Lord in whom they had put their faith. [24]Then they traveled through Pisidia and reached Pamphylia. [25]After proclaiming the word at Perga they went down to Attalia. [26]From there they sailed to Antioch, where they had been commended to the grace of God for the work they had now accomplished. [27]And when they arrived, they called the church together and reported what God had done with them and how he had opened the door of faith to the Gentiles.

Responsorial Psalm: Psalms 145:8-9, 10-11, 12-13

R. [(cf. 1)] I will praise your name for ever, my king and my God. or: *R. Alleluia.*
[8] The LORD is gracious and merciful,
    slow to anger and of great kindness.
[9] The LORD is good to all
    and compassionate toward all his works.
R. I will praise your name for ever, my king and my God. or: *R. Alleluia.*
[10] Let all your works give you thanks, O LORD,
    and let your faithful ones bless you.
[11] Let them discourse of the glory of your kingdom
    and speak of your might.
R. I will praise your name for ever, my king and my God. or: *R. Alleluia.*
[12] Let them make known your might to the
    children of Adam,

and the glorious splendor of your kingdom.
¹³ Your kingdom is a kingdom for all ages,
   and your dominion endures through all
      generations.
R. I will praise your name for ever, my king and
     my God. or: **R. Alleluia.**

Second Reading: Revelation 21:1-5A

[1] Then I, John, saw a new heaven and a new earth. The former heaven and the former earth had passed away, and the sea was no more. [2] I also saw the holy city, a new Jerusalem, coming down out of heaven from God, prepared as a bride adorned for her husband. [3] I heard a loud voice from the throne saying, "Behold, God's dwelling is with the human race. He will dwell with them and they will be his people and God himself will always be with them as their God. [4] He will wipe every tear from their eyes, and there shall be no more death or mourning, wailing or pain, for the old order has passed away."

[5] The One who sat on the throne said, "Behold, I make all things new."

Alleluia: John 13:34

R. Alleluia, alleluia.
[34] I give you a new commandment, says the
     Lord:
love one another as I have loved you.
R. Alleluia, alleluia.

Gospel: John 13:31-33A, 34-35

[31] When Judas had left them, Jesus said, "Now is the Son of Man glorified, and God is glorified in him. [32] If God is glorified in him, God will also glorify him in himself, and God will glorify him at once. [33A] My children, I will be with you only a little while longer. [34] I give you a new commandment: love one another. As I have loved you, so you also should love one another. [35] This is how all will know that you are my disciples, if you have love for one another."

Sunday May 25, 2025
Sixth Sunday of Easter, Year C
First Reading: Acts 15:1-2, 22-29

[1] Some who had come down from Judea were instructing the brothers, "Unless you are circumcised according to the Mosaic practice, you cannot be saved." [2] Because there arose no little dissension and debate by Paul and Barnabas with them, it was decided that Paul, Barnabas, and some of the others should go up to Jerusalem to the apostles and elders about this question.

²²The apostles and elders, in agreement with the whole church, decided to choose representatives and to send them to Antioch with Paul and Barnabas. The ones chosen were Judas, who was called Barsabbas, and Silas, leaders among the brothers. ²³This is the letter delivered by them:

"The apostles and the elders, your brothers, to the brothers in Antioch, Syria, and Cilicia of Gentile origin: greetings. ²⁴Since we have heard that some of our number who went out without any mandate from us have upset you with their teachings and disturbed your peace of mind, ²⁵we have with one accord decided to choose representatives and to send them to you along with our beloved Barnabas and Paul, ²⁶who have dedicated their lives to the name of our Lord Jesus Christ. ²⁷So we are sending Judas and Silas who will also convey this same message by word of mouth: ²⁸'It is the decision of the Holy Spirit and of us not to place on you any burden beyond these necessities, ²⁹namely, to abstain from meat sacrificed to idols, from blood, from meats of strangled animals, and from unlawful marriage. If you keep free of these, you will be doing what is right. Farewell.'"

Responsorial Psalm: Psalms 67:2-3, 5, 6, 8

R. ⁽⁴⁾ *O God, let all the nations praise you!* or: *R. Alleluia.*

² May God have pity on us and bless us;
    may he let his face shine upon us.
³ So may your way be known upon earth;
    among all nations, your salvation.

R. *O God, let all the nations praise you!* or: *R. Alleluia.*

⁵ May the nations be glad and exult
    because you rule the peoples in equity;
    the nations on the earth you guide.

R. *O God, let all the nations praise you!* or: *R. Alleluia.*

⁶ May the peoples praise you, O God;
    may all the peoples praise you!
⁸ May God bless us,
    and may all the ends of the earth fear
      him!

R. *O God, let all the nations praise you!* or: *R. Alleluia.*

Second Reading: Revelation 21:10-14, 22-23

¹⁰The angel took me in spirit to a great, high mountain and showed me the holy city Jerusalem coming down out of heaven from God. ¹¹ It gleamed with the splendor of God. Its radiance was like that of a precious stone, like a jasper, clear as crystal. ¹² It had a massive, high wall, with twelve gates where twelve angels were stationed and on which names were inscribed, the names of the twelve tribes of the Israelites. ¹³There were three gates facing east, three north, three south, and three west. ¹⁴The wall of the city had twelve courses of stones as its foundation, on which were inscribed the twelve names of the twelve apostles of the Lamb.

[22]I saw no temple in the city for its temple is the Lord God Almighty and the Lamb. [23]The city had no need of sun or moon to shine on it, for the glory of God gave it light, and its lamp was the Lamb.

Alleluia: John 14:23

R. Alleluia, alleluia.
[23] Whoever loves me will keep my word,
      says the Lord,
and my Father will love him and we will
      come to him.
R. Alleluia, alleluia.

Gospel: John 14:23-29

[23]Jesus said to his disciples: "Whoever loves me will keep my word, and my Father will love him, and we will come to him and make our dwelling with him. [24]Whoever does not love me does not keep my words, yet the word you hear is not mine but that of the Father who sent me.

[25] "I have told you this while I am with you. [26]The Advocate, the Holy Spirit, whom the Father will send in my name, will teach you everything and remind you of all that I told you. [27]Peace I leave with you; my peace I give to you. Not as the world gives do I give it to you. Do not let your hearts be troubled or afraid. [28]You heard me tell you, 'I am going away and I will come back to you.' If you loved me, you would rejoice that I am going to the Father; for the Father is greater than I. [29]And now I have told you this before it happens, so that when it happens you may believe."

JUNE 2025
Sunday June 1, 2025
Solemnity of the Ascension of the Lord
First Reading: Acts 1:1-11

[1] In the first book, Theophilus, I dealt with all that Jesus did and taught [2] until the day he was taken up, after giving instructions through the Holy Spirit to the apostles whom he had chosen. [3] He presented himself alive to them by many proofs after he had suffered, appearing to them during forty days and speaking about the kingdom of God. [4] While meeting with them, he enjoined them not to depart from Jerusalem, but to wait for "the promise of the Father about which you have heard me speak; [5] for John baptized with water, but in a few days you will be baptized with the Holy Spirit."

[6] When they had gathered together they asked him, "Lord, are you at this time going to restore the kingdom to Israel?" [7] He answered them, "It is not for you to know the times or seasons that the Father has established by his own authority. [8] But you will receive power when the Holy Spirit comes upon you, and you will be my witnesses in Jerusalem, throughout Judea and Samaria, and to the ends of the earth." [9] When he had said this, as they were looking on, he was lifted up, and a cloud took him from their

sight. [10] While they were looking intently at the sky as he was going, suddenly two men dressed in white garments stood beside them. [11] They said, "Men of Galilee, why are you standing there looking at the sky? This Jesus who has been taken up from you into heaven will return in the same way as you have seen him going into heaven."

Responsorial Psalm: Psalms 47:2-3, 6-7, 8-9

R. [(6)] ***God mounts his throne to shouts of joy: a***
                 blare of trumpets for the Lord.

or: ***Alleluia.***

[2] All you peoples, clap your hands,
      shout to God with cries of gladness,
[3] For the LORD, the Most High, the awesome,
      is the great king over all the earth.

R. *God mounts his throne to shouts of joy: a*
                 blare of trumpets for the Lord.

or: ***Alleluia.***

[6] God mounts his throne amid shouts of joy;
      the LORD, amid trumpet blasts.
[7] Sing praise to God, sing praise;
      sing praise to our king, sing praise.

R. *God mounts his throne to shouts of joy: a*
                 blare of trumpets for the Lord.

or: ***Alleluia.***

[8] For king of all the earth is God;
      sing hymns of praise.
[9] God reigns over the nations,
      God sits upon his holy throne.

R. *God mounts his throne to shouts of joy: a*
                 blare of trumpets for the Lord.

or: ***Alleluia.***

Second Reading: Ephesians 1:17-23

Brothers and sisters: [17] May the God of our Lord Jesus Christ, the Father of glory, give you a Spirit of wisdom and revelation resulting in knowledge of him. [18] May the eyes of your hearts be enlightened, that you may know what is the hope that belongs to his call, what are the riches of glory in his inheritance among the holy ones, [19] and what is the surpassing greatness of his power for us who believe, in accord with the exercise of his great might, [20] which he worked in Christ, raising him from the dead and seating him at his right hand in the heavens, [21] far above every principality, authority, power, and dominion, and every name that is named not only in this age but also in the one to come. [22] And he put all things beneath his feet and gave him as head over all things to the church, which is his body, the fullness of the one who fills all things in every way.

Hebrews 9:24-28; 10:19-23

[24]For Christ did not enter into a sanctuary made by hands, a copy of the true one, but heaven itself, that he might now appear before God on our behalf. [25]Not that he might offer himself repeatedly, as the high priest enters each year into the sanctuary with blood that is not his own; [26] if that were so, he would have had to suffer repeatedly from the foundation of the world. But now once for all he has appeared at the end of the ages to take away sin by his sacrifice. [27]Just as it is appointed that human beings die once, and after this the judgment, [28] so also Christ, offered once to take away the sins of many, will appear a second time, not to take away sin but to bring salvation to those who eagerly await him. [19]Therefore, brothers, since through the blood of Jesus we have confidence of entrance into the sanctuary [20] by the new and living way he opened for us through the veil, that is, his flesh, [21] and since we have "a great priest over the house of God," [22] let us approach with a sincere heart and in absolute trust, with our hearts sprinkled clean from an evil conscience and our bodies washed in pure water. [23] Let us hold unwaveringly to our confession that gives us hope, for he who made the promise is trustworthy.

Alleluia: Matthew 28:19A, 20B
R. Alleluia, alleluia.
[19A] Go and teach all nations, says the Lord;
[20B] I am with you always, until the end of the
world.
R. Alleluia, alleluia.

Gospel: Luke 24:46-53

[46]Jesus said to his disciples: "Thus it is written that the Christ would suffer and rise from the dead on the third day [47]and that repentance, for the forgiveness of sins, would be preached in his name to all the nations, beginning from Jerusalem. [48]You are witnesses of these things. [49]And behold I am sending the promise of my Father upon you; but stay in the city until you are clothed with power from on high."

[50]Then he led them out as far as Bethany, raised his hands, and blessed them. [51]As he blessed them he parted from them and was taken up to heaven. [52]They did him homage and then returned to Jerusalem with great joy, [53] and they were continually in the temple praising God.

Sunday June 8, 2025
Pentecost Sunday

First Reading: Acts 2:1-11

[1] When the time for Pentecost was fulfilled, they were all in one place together. [2] And suddenly there came from the sky a noise like a strong driving wind, and it filled the entire house in which they were. [3] Then there appeared to them tongues as of fire, which parted and came to rest on each one of them. [4] And they were all filled with the Holy Spirit and began to speak in different tongues, as the Spirit enabled them to proclaim.

[5] Now there were devout Jews from every nation under heaven staying in Jerusalem. [6] At this sound, they gathered in a large crowd, but they were confused because each one heard them speaking in his own language. [7] They were astounded, and in amazement, they asked, "Are not all these people who are speaking Galileans? [8] Then how does each of us hear them in his native language? [9] We are Parthians, Medes, and Elamites, inhabitants of Mesopotamia, Judea and Cappadocia, Pontus and Asia, [10] Phrygia and Pamphylia, Egypt and the districts of Libya near Cyrene, as well as travelers from Rome, [11] both Jews and converts to Judaism, Cretans and Arabs, yet we hear them speaking in our own tongues of the mighty acts of God."

Responsorial Psalm: Psalms 104:1, 24, 29-30, 31, 34

R. [(cf. 30)] *Lord, send out your Spirit, and renew the*
face of the earth. or: *Alleluia.*

[1] Bless the LORD, O my soul!
    O LORD, my God, you are great indeed!
[24] How manifold are your works, O LORD!
    The earth is full of your creatures;

R. *Lord, send out your Spirit, and renew the face*
of the earth. or: *Alleluia.*

[29] If you take away their breath, they perish
    and return to their dust.
[30] When you send forth your spirit, they are
        created,
    and you renew the face of the earth.

R. *Lord, send out your Spirit, and renew the face*
of the earth. or: *Alleluia.*

[31] May the glory of the LORD endure forever;
    may the LORD be glad in his works!
[34] Pleasing to him be my theme;
    I will be glad in the LORD.

R. *Lord, send out your Spirit, and renew the face*
of the earth. or: *Alleluia.*

Second Reading: 1 Corinthians 12:3B-7, 12-13

Brothers and sisters: [3B] No one can say, "Jesus is Lord," except by the Holy Spirit. [4] There are different kinds of spiritual gifts but the same Spirit; [5] there are different forms of service but the same Lord; [6] there are different workings but the same God who produces all of them in everyone. [7] To each individual the manifestation of the Spirit is given for some benefit.

    [12] As a body is one though it has many parts, and all the parts of the body, though many, are one body, so also Christ. [13] For in one Spirit we were all baptized into one body, whether Jews or Greeks, slaves or free persons, and we were all given to drink of one Spirit.

Or Romans 8:8-17

Brothers and sisters: [8]Those who are in the flesh cannot please God. [9]But you are not in the flesh; on the contrary, you are in the spirit, if only the Spirit of God dwells in you. Whoever does not have the Spirit of Christ does not belong to him. [10]But if Christ is in you, although the body is dead because of sin, the spirit is alive because of righteousness. [11]If the Spirit of the one who raised Jesus from the dead dwells in you, the one who raised Christ from the dead will give life to your mortal bodies also, through his Spirit that dwells in you. [12]Consequently, brothers and sisters, we are not debtors to the flesh, to live according to the flesh. [13]For if you live according to the flesh, you will die, but if by the Spirit you put to death the deeds of the body, you will live.

[14]For those who are led by the Spirit of God are sons of God. [15]For you did not receive a spirit of slavery to fall back into fear, but you received a Spirit of adoption, through whom we cry, "Abba, Father!" [16]The Spirit himself bears witness with our spirit that we are children of God, [17]and if children, then heirs, heirs of God and joint heirs with Christ, if only we suffer with him so that we may also be glorified with him.

Sequence - *Veni, Sancte Spiritus*

Come, Holy Spirit, come!
And from your celestial home
Shed a ray of light divine!
Come, Father of the poor!
Come, source of all our store!
Come, within our bosoms shine.
You, of comforters the best;
You, the soul's most welcome guest;
Sweet refreshment here below;
In our labor, rest most sweet;
Grateful coolness in the heat;
Solace in the midst of woe.
O most blessed Light divine,
Shine within these hearts of yours,
And our inmost being fill!
Where you are not, we have naught,
Nothing good in deed or thought,
Nothing free from taint of ill.
Heal our wounds, our strength renew;
On our dryness pour your dew;
Wash the stains of guilt away:
Bend the stubborn heart and will;
Melt the frozen, warm the chill;
Guide the steps that go astray.
On the faithful, who adore

And confess you, evermore
In your sevenfold gift descend;
Give them virtue's sure reward;
Give them your salvation, Lord;
Give them joys that never end. Amen.
Alleluia.

Alleluia
R. Alleluia, alleluia.
Come, Holy Spirit, fill the hearts of your
        faithful
and kindle in them the fire of your love.
R. Alleluia, alleluia.

Gospel: John 20:19-23
[19] On the evening of that first day of the week, when the doors were locked, where the disciples were, for fear of the Jews, Jesus came and stood in their midst and said to them, "Peace be with you." [20] When he had said this, he showed them his hands and his side. The disciples rejoiced when they saw the Lord. [21] Jesus said to them again, "Peace be with you. As the Father has sent me, so I send you." [22] And when he had said this, he breathed on them and said to them, "Receive the Holy Spirit. [23] Whose sins you forgive are forgiven them, and whose sins you retain are retained."

Or John 14:15-16, 23B-26
Jesus said to his disciples: [15]"If you love me, you will keep my commandments. [16]And I will ask the Father, and he will give you another Advocate to be with you always.

[23B]"Whoever loves me will keep my word, and my Father will love him, and we will come to him and make our dwelling with him. [24]Those who do not love me do not keep my words; yet the word you hear is not mine but that of the Father who sent me.

[25]"I have told you this while I am with you. [26]The Advocate, the Holy Spirit whom the Father will send in my name, will teach you everything and remind you of all that I told you."

The Solemnity of the Most Holy Trinity, Year C
First Reading: Proverbs 8:22-31
Thus says the wisdom of God:

[22]"The LORD possessed me, the beginning of his
        ways,
    the forerunner of his prodigies of long
        ago;
[23] from of old I was poured forth,
    at the first, before the earth.

²⁴When there were no depths I was brought
>   forth,
>   when there were no fountains or springs
>   of water;
²⁵before the mountains were settled into
>   place,
>   before the hills, I was brought forth;
²⁶ while as yet the earth and fields were not
>   made,
>   nor the first clods of the world.

²⁷ "When the Lord established the heavens I
>   was there,
>   when he marked out the vault over the
>   face of the deep;
²⁸ when he made firm the skies above,
>   when he fixed fast the foundations of the
>   earth;
²⁹ when he set for the sea its limit,
>   so that the waters should not transgress
>   his command;
³⁰ then was I beside him as his craftsman,
>   and I was his delight day by day,
playing before him all the while,
>   ³¹playing on the surface of his earth;
>   and I found delight in the human race."

Responsorial Psalm: Psalms 8:4-5, 6-7, 8-9

R. *(2a)* ***O Lord, our God, how wonderful your***
> ***name in all the earth!***

⁴When I behold your heavens, the work of
>   your fingers,
>   the moon and the stars which you set in
>   place—
⁵ What is man that you should be mindful of
>   him,
>   or the son of man that you should care
>   for him?

R. *O Lord, our God, how wonderful your name in*
> ***all the earth!***

⁶ You have made him little less than the
>   angels,
>   and crowned him with glory and honor.
⁷ You have given him rule over the works of
>   your hands,

putting all things under his feet:

R. O Lord, our God, how wonderful your name in
all the earth!

[8] All sheep and oxen,
yes, and the beasts of the field,
[9] The birds of the air, the fishes of the sea,
and whatever swims the paths of the
seas.

R. O Lord, our God, how wonderful your name in
all the earth!

Second Reading: Romans 5:1-5

Brothers and sisters: [1]Therefore, since we have been justified by faith, we have peace with God through our Lord Jesus Christ, [2]through whom we have gained access by faith to this grace in which we stand, and we boast in hope of the glory of God. [3]Not only that, but we even boast of our afflictions, knowing that affliction produces endurance, [4]and endurance, proven character, and proven character, hope, [5]and hope does not disappoint, because the love of God has been poured out into our hearts through the Holy Spirit that has been given to us.

Alleluia: cf. Revelation 1:8
R. Alleluia, alleluia.

[8] Glory to the Father, the Son, and the Holy
Spirit;
to God who is, who was, and who is to come.

R. Alleluia, alleluia.

Gospel: John 16:12-15

Jesus said to his disciples: [12]"I have much more to tell you, but you cannot bear it now. [13]But when he comes, the Spirit of truth, he will guide you to all truth. He will not speak on his own, but he will speak what he hears, and will declare to you the things that are coming. [14]He will glorify me because he will take from what is mine and declare it to you. [15]Everything that the Father has is mine; for this reason I told you that he will take from what is mine and declare it to you."

Sunday June 22, 2025

Solemnity of Body and Blood of Christ (*Corpus Christi*)
First Reading: Genesis 14:18-20

[18] In those days, Melchizedek, king of Salem, brought out bread and wine, and being a priest of God Most High, [19]he blessed Abram with these words:

"Blessed be Abram by God Most High,
the creator of heaven and earth;
[20]and blessed be God Most High,
who delivered your foes into your hand."

Then Abram gave him a tenth of everything.

Responsorial Psalm: Psalms 110:1, 2, 3, 4

R. *(4b)* **You are a priest for ever, in the line of Melchizedek.**

[1] The LORD said to my Lord: "Sit at my right hand
till I make your enemies your footstool."

R. You are a priest for ever, in the line of Melchizedek.

[2] The sceptre of your power the LORD will stretch forth from Zion:
"Rule in the midst of your enemies."

R. You are a priest for ever, in the line of Melchizedek.

[3] "Yours is princely power in the day of your birth, in holy splendor;
before the daystar, like the dew, I have begotten you."

R. You are a priest for ever, in the line of Melchizedek.

[4] The LORD has sworn, and he will not repent:
"You are a priest forever, according to the order of Melchizedek."

R. You are a priest for ever, in the line of Melchizedek.

Second Reading: 1 Corinthians 11:23-26

Brothers and sisters: [23] I received from the Lord what I also handed on to you that the Lord Jesus, on the night he was handed over, took bread, [24] and, after he had given thanks, broke it and said, "This is my body that is for you. Do this in remembrance of me." [25] In the same way also the cup, after supper, saying, "This cup is the new covenant in my blood. Do this, as often as you drink it, in remembrance of me." [26] For as often as you eat this bread and drink the cup, you proclaim the death of the Lord until he comes.

Sequence - *Lauda Sion*

Laud, O Zion, your salvation,
Laud with hymns of exultation,
Christ, your king and shepherd true:

Bring him all the praise you know,
He is more than you bestow.
Never can you reach his due.

Special theme for glad thanksgiving
Is the quick'ning and the living
Bread today before you set:

From his hands of old partaken,
As we know, by faith unshaken,
Where the Twelve at supper met.

Full and clear ring out your chanting,
Joy nor sweetest grace be wanting,
From your heart let praises burst:

For today the feast is holden,
When the institution olden
Of that supper was rehearsed.

Here the new law's new oblation,
By the new king's revelation,
Ends the form of ancient rite:

Now the new the old effaces,
Truth away the shadow chases,
Light dispels the gloom of night.

What he did at supper seated,
Christ ordained to be repeated,
His memorial ne'er to cease:

And his rule for guidance taking,
Bread and wine we hallow, making
Thus our sacrifice of peace.
This the truth each Christian learns,
Bread into his flesh he turns,
To his precious blood the wine:

Sight has fail'd, nor thought conceives,
But a dauntless faith believes,
Resting on a pow'r divine.

Here beneath these signs are hidden
Priceless things to sense forbidden;
Sign, not things are all we see:

Blood is poured and flesh is broken,

Yet in either wondrous token
Christ entire we know to be.

Whoso of this food partakes,
Does not rend the Lord nor breaks;
Christ is whole to all that tastes:

Thousands are, as one, receivers,
One, as thousands of believers,
Eats of him who cannot waste.

Bad and good the feast are sharing,
Of what divers dooms preparing,
Endless death, or endless life.

Life to these, to those damnation,
See how like participation
Is with unlike issues rife.

When the sacrament is broken,
Doubt not, but believe 'tis spoken,
That each sever'd outward token
doth the very whole contain.

Nought the precious gift divides,
Breaking but the sign betides
Jesus still the same abides,
still unbroken does remain.

The shorter form of the sequence begins here.

Lo! the angel's food is given
To the pilgrim who has striven;
See the children's bread from heaven,
which on dogs may not be spent.

Truth the ancient types fulfilling,
Isaac bound, a victim willing,
Paschal lamb, its lifeblood spilling,
manna to the fathers sent.

Very bread, good shepherd, tend us,
Jesu, of your love befriend us,
You refresh us, you defend us,
Your eternal goodness send us

In the land of life to see.

You who all things can and know,
Who on earth such food bestow,
Grant us with your saints, though lowest,
Where the heav'nly feast you show,
Fellow heirs and guests to be. Amen.
 Alleluia.

Alleluia: John 6:51
R. Alleluia, alleluia.
[51] I am the living bread that came down from
      heaven, says the Lord;
whoever eats this bread will live forever.
R. Alleluia, alleluia.

Gospel: Luke 9:11B-17
[11B] Jesus spoke to the crowds about the kingdom of God, and he healed those who needed to be cured. [12] As the day was drawing to a close, the Twelve approached him and said, "Dismiss the crowd so that they can go to the surrounding villages and farms and find lodging and provisions; for we are in a deserted place here." [13] He said to them, "Give them some food yourselves." They replied, "Five loaves and two fish are all we have, unless we ourselves go and buy food for all these people." [14] Now the men there numbered about five thousand. Then he said to his disciples, "Have them sit down in groups of about fifty." [15] They did so and made them all sit down. [16] Then taking the five loaves and the two fish, and looking up to heaven, he said the blessing over them, broke them, and gave them to the disciples to set before the crowd. [17]They all ate and were satisfied. And when the leftover fragments were picked up, they filled twelve wicker baskets.

Sunday June 29, 2025
Solemnity of Saints Peter and Paul, Apostles
First Reading: Acts 12:1-11
[1] In those days, King Herod laid hands upon some members of the Church to harm them. [2] He had James, the brother of John, killed by the sword, [3] and when he saw that this was pleasing to the Jews he proceeded to arrest Peter also. —It was the feast of Unleavened Bread.— [4] He had him taken into custody and put in prison under the guard of four squads of four soldiers each. He intended to bring him before the people after Passover. [5] Peter thus was being kept in prison, but prayer by the Church was fervently being made to God on his behalf.

[6] On the very night before Herod was to bring him to trial, Peter, secured by double chains, was sleeping between two soldiers, while outside the door guards kept watch on the prison. [7] Suddenly the angel of the Lord stood by him, and a light shone in the cell. He tapped Peter on the side and awakened him, saying, "Get up quickly." The chains fell from his wrists. [8] The angel said to him, "Put on your belt

and your sandals." He did so. Then he said to him, "Put on your cloak and follow me." [9] So he followed him out, not realizing that what was happening through the angel was real; he thought he was seeing a vision. [10] They passed the first guard, then the second, and came to the iron gate leading out to the city, which opened for them by itself. They emerged and made their way down an alley, and suddenly the angel left him. [11] Then Peter recovered his senses and said, "Now I know for certain that the Lord sent his angel and rescued me from the hand of Herod and from all that the Jewish people had been expecting."

Responsorial Psalm: Psalms 34:2-3, 4-5, 6-7, 8-9

R. [(5)] *The angel of the Lord will rescue those who
        fear him.*

[2] I will bless the LORD at all times;
    his praise shall be ever in my mouth.
[3] Let my soul glory in the LORD;
    the lowly will hear me and be glad.

R. *The angel of the Lord will rescue those who
        fear him.*

[4] Glorify the LORD with me,
    let us together extol his name.
[5] I sought the LORD, and he answered me
    and delivered me from all my fears.

R. *The angel of the Lord will rescue those who
        fear him.*

[6] Look to him that you may be radiant with
        joy,
    and your faces may not blush with
        shame.
[7] When the poor one called out, the LORD
        heard,
    and from all his distress he saved him.

R. *The angel of the Lord will rescue those who
        fear him.*

[8] The angel of the LORD encamps
    around those who fear him, and delivers
        them.
[9] Taste and see how good the LORD is;
    blessed the man who takes refuge in him.

R. *The angel of the Lord will rescue those who
        fear him.*

Second Reading: 2 Timothy 4:6-8, 17-18

[6] I, Paul, am already being poured out like a libation, and the time of my departure is at hand. [7] I have competed well; I have finished the race; I have kept the faith. [8] From now

on the crown of righteousness awaits me, which the Lord, the just judge, will award to me on that day, and not only to me, but to all who have longed for his appearance.

[17] The Lord stood by me and gave me strength, so that through me the proclamation might be completed and all the Gentiles might hear it. And I was rescued from the lion's mouth. [18] The Lord will rescue me from every evil threat and will bring me safe to his heavenly Kingdom. To him be glory forever and ever. Amen.

Alleluia: Matthew 16:18

R. Alleluia, alleluia.

[18] You are Peter and upon this rock I will build
        my Church,
and the gates of the netherworld shall not
           prevail against it.

R. Alleluia, alleluia.

Gospel: Matthew 16:13-19

[13] When Jesus went into the region of Caesarea Philippi he asked his disciples, "Who do people say that the Son of Man is?" [14] They replied, "Some say John the Baptist, others Elijah, still others Jeremiah or one of the prophets." [15] He said to them, "But who do you say that I am?" [16] Simon Peter said in reply, "You are the Christ, the Son of the living God." [17] Jesus said to him in reply, "Blessed are you, Simon son of Jonah. For flesh and blood has not revealed this to you, but my heavenly Father. [18] And so I say to you, you are Peter, and upon this rock I will build my Church, and the gates of the netherworld shall not prevail against it. [19] I will give you the keys to the Kingdom of heaven. Whatever you bind on earth shall be bound in heaven; and whatever you loose on earth shall be loosed in heaven."

JULY 2025
Sunday July 6, 2025

Fourteenth Sunday in Ordinary Time, Year C

First Reading: Isaiah 66:10-14C

Thus says the LORD:

[10] Rejoice with Jerusalem and be glad because
        of her,
    all you who love her;
exult, exult with her,
    all you who were mourning over her!
Oh, that you may suck fully
    of the milk of her comfort,
[11] that you may nurse with delight
    at her abundant breasts!
    [12] For thus says the LORD:
Lo, I will spread prosperity over Jerusalem

like a river,
and the wealth of the nations like an
overflowing torrent.
As nurslings, you shall be carried in her
arms,
and fondled in her lap;
[13]as a mother comforts her child,
so will I comfort you;
in Jerusalem, you shall find your comfort.

[14C] When you see this, your heart shall rejoice
and your bodies flourish like the grass;
the LORD's power shall be known to his
servants.

Responsorial Psalm: Psalms 66:1-3, 4-5, 6-7, 16, 20

R. [(1)] *Let all the earth cry out to God with joy.*
[2] Shout joyfully to God, all the earth,
sing praise to the glory of his name;
proclaim his glorious praise.
[3] Say to God, "How tremendous are your
deeds!"
R. *Let all the earth cry out to God with joy.*
[4] "Let all on earth worship and sing praise to
you,
sing praise to your name!"
[5] Come and see the works of God,
his tremendous deeds among the
children of Adam.
R. *Let all the earth cry out to God with joy.*
[6] He has changed the sea into dry land;
through the river they passed on foot;
therefore let us rejoice in him.
[7] He rules by his might forever.
R. *Let all the earth cry out to God with joy.*
[16] Hear now, all you who fear God,
while I declare what he has done for me.
[20] Blessed be God who refused me not
my prayer or his kindness!
R. *Let all the earth cry out to God with joy.*

Second Reading: Galatians 6:14-18

Brothers and sisters: [14]May I never boast except in the cross of our Lord Jesus Christ, through which the world has been crucified to me, and I to the world. [15]For neither does circumcision mean anything, nor does uncircumcision, but only a new creation. [16]Peace and mercy be to all who follow this rule and to the Israel of God.

[17]From now on, let no one make troubles for me; for I bear the marks of Jesus on my body.

[18]The grace of our Lord Jesus Christ be with your spirit, brothers and sisters. Amen.

Alleluia: Colossians 3:15a, 16a
R. Alleluia, alleluia.
[15A] Let the peace of Christ control your hearts;
[16A] let the word of Christ dwell in you richly.
R. Alleluia, alleluia.

Gospel: Luke 10:1-12, 17-20
[1] At that time the Lord appointed seventy-two others whom he sent ahead of him in pairs to every town and place he intended to visit. [2]He said to them, "The harvest is abundant but the laborers are few; so ask the master of the harvest to send out laborers for his harvest. [3]Go on your way; behold, I am sending you like lambs among wolves. [4]Carry no money bag, no sack, no sandals; and greet no one along the way. [5] Into whatever house you enter, first say, 'Peace to this household.' [6] If a peaceful person lives there, your peace will rest on him; but if not, it will return to you. [7]Stay in the same house and eat and drink what is offered to you, for the laborer deserves his payment. Do not move about from one house to another. [8]Whatever town you enter and they welcome you, eat what is set before you, [9]cure the sick in it and say to them, 'The kingdom of God is at hand for you.' [10]Whatever town you enter and they do not receive you, go out into the streets and say, [11]'The dust of your town that clings to our feet, even that we shake off against you.' Yet know this: the kingdom of God is at hand. [12] I tell you, it will be more tolerable for Sodom on that day than for that town."

[17]The seventy-two returned rejoicing, and said, "Lord, even the demons are subject to us because of your name." [18]Jesus said, "I have observed Satan fall like lightning from the sky. [19] Behold, I have given you the power to 'tread upon serpents' and scorpions and upon the full force of the enemy and nothing will harm you. [20] Nevertheless, do not rejoice because the spirits are subject to you, but rejoice because your names are written in heaven."

Or Luke 10:1-9
[1]At that time the Lord appointed seventy-two others whom he sent ahead of him in pairs to every town and place he intended to visit. [2] He said to them, "The harvest is abundant but the laborers are few; so ask the master of the harvest to send out laborers for his harvest. [3] Go on your way; behold, I am sending you like lambs among wolves. [4]Carry no money bag, no sack, no sandals; and greet no one along the way. [5] Into whatever house you enter, first say, 'Peace to this household.' [6] If a peaceful person lives there, your peace will rest on him; but if not, it will return to you. [7]Stay in the same house and eat and drink what is offered to you, for the

laborer deserves his payment. Do not move about from one house to another. [8]Whatever town you enter and they welcome you, eat what is set before you, [9] cure the sick in it and say to them, 'The kingdom of God is at hand for you.'"

Fifteenth Sunday in Ordinary Time, Year C
First Reading: Deuteronomy 30:10-14

Moses said to the people: [10]"If only you would heed the voice of the LORD, your God, and keep his commandments and statutes that are written in this book of the law, when you return to the LORD, your God, with all your heart and all your soul.

[11]"For this command that I enjoin on you today is not too mysterious and remote for you. [12] It is not up in the sky, that you should say, 'Who will go up in the sky to get it for us and tell us of it, that we may carry it out?' [13] Nor is it across the sea, that you should say, 'Who will cross the sea to get it for us and tell us of it, that we may carry it out?' [14] No, it is something very near to you, already in your mouths and in your hearts; you have only to carry it out."

Responsorial Psalm: Psalms 69:14, 17, 30-31, 33-34, 36, 37

R. [(cf. 33)] *Turn to the Lord in your need, and you*
will live.

[14] I pray to you, O LORD,
    for the time of your favor, O God!
In your great kindness answer me
    with your constant help.
[17] Answer me, O LORD, for bounteous is
        your kindness:
    in your great mercy turn toward me.
R. Turn to the Lord in your need, and you
        will live.

[30] I am afflicted and in pain;
    let your saving help, O God, protect
        me.
[31] I will praise the name of God in song,
    and I will glorify him with
        thanksgiving.
R. Turn to the Lord in your need, and you
        will live.

[33] "See, you lowly ones, and be glad;
    you who seek God, may your hearts
        revive!
[34] For the LORD hears the poor,
    and his own who are in bonds he
        spurns not."
R. Turn to the Lord in your need, and you
        will live.

³⁶ For God will save Zion
     and rebuild the cities of Judah.
³⁷ The descendants of his servants shall
          inherit it,
     and those who love his name shall
          inhabit it.
*R. Turn to the Lord in your need, and you
     will live.*

Or Psalms 19:8, 9, 10, 11
R.^(9a) Your words, Lord, are Spirit and life.
⁸The law of the LORD is perfect,
     refreshing the soul;
the decree of the LORD is trustworthy,
     giving wisdom to the simple.
R. Your words, Lord, are Spirit and life.
⁹ The precepts of the LORD are right,
     rejoicing the heart;
the command of the LORD is clear,
     enlightening the eye.
R. Your words, Lord, are Spirit and life.
¹⁰ The fear of the LORD is pure,
     enduring forever;
the ordinances of the LORD are true,
     all of them just.
R. Your words, Lord, are Spirit and life.
¹¹ They are more precious than gold,
     than a heap of purest gold;
sweeter also than syrup
     or honey from the comb.
R. Your words, Lord, are Spirit and life.

Second Reading: Colossians 1:15-20
¹⁵Christ Jesus is the image of the invisible God, the firstborn of all creation. ¹⁶For in him were created all things in heaven and on earth, the visible and the invisible, whether thrones or dominions or principalities or powers; all things were created through him and for him. ¹⁷He is before all things, and in him, all things hold together. ¹⁸ He is the head of the body, the church. He is the beginning, the firstborn from the dead, that in all things he himself might be preeminent. ¹⁹ For in him all the fullness was pleased to dwell, ²⁰and through him to reconcile all things for him, making peace by the blood of his cross through him, whether those on earth or those in heaven.

Alleluia: cf. John 6:63C, 68C

R. Alleluia, alleluia.
[63C] Your words, Lord, are Spirit and life;
[68C] you have the words of everlasting life.
R. Alleluia, alleluia.

Gospel: Luke 10:25-37

[25]There was a scholar of the law who stood up to test Jesus and said, "Teacher, what must I do to inherit eternal life?" [26]Jesus said to him, "What is written in the law? How do you read it?" [27] He said in reply, *You shall love the Lord, your God, with all your heart, with all your being, with all your strength,*
and with all your mind, and your neighbor as yourself." [28]He replied to him, "You have answered correctly; do this and you will live."

[29]But because he wished to justify himself, he said to Jesus, "And who is my neighbor?" [30]Jesus replied, "A man fell victim to robbers as he went down from Jerusalem to Jericho. They stripped and beat him and went off leaving him half-dead. [31]A priest happened to be going down that road, but when he saw him, he passed by on the opposite side. [32]Likewise a Levite came to the place, and when he saw him, he passed by on the opposite side. [33]But a Samaritan traveler who came upon him was moved with compassion at the sight. [34]He approached the victim, poured oil and wine over his wounds and bandaged them. Then he lifted him up on his own animal, took him to an inn, and cared for him. [35]The next day he took out two silver coins and gave them to the innkeeper with the instruction, 'Take care of him. If you spend more than what I have given you, I shall repay you on my way back.' [36]Which of these three, in your opinion, was a neighbor to the robbers' victim?" [37]He answered, "The one who treated him with mercy." Jesus said to him, "Go and do likewise."

Sunday July 20, 2025
Sixteenth Sunday in Ordinary Time, Year C
First Reading: Genesis 18:1-10A

[1]The LORD appeared to Abraham by the terebinth of Mamre, as he sat in the entrance of his tent, while the day was growing hot. [2]Looking up, Abraham saw three men standing nearby. When he saw them, he ran from the entrance of the tent to greet them; and bowing to the ground, he said: [3] "Sir, if I may ask you this favor, please do not go on past your servant. [4]Let some water be brought, that you may bathe your feet, and then rest yourselves under the tree. [5]Now that you have come this close to your servant, let me bring you a little food, that you may refresh yourselves; and afterward you may go on your way." The men replied, "Very well, do as you have said."

[6]Abraham hastened into the tent and told Sarah, "Quick, three measures of fine flour! Knead it and make rolls." [7]He ran to the herd, picked out a tender, choice steer, and gave it to a servant, who quickly prepared it. [8]Then Abraham got some curds and milk, as well as the steer that had been prepared, and set these before the three men; and he waited on them under the tree while they ate.

[9]They asked Abraham, "Where is your wife Sarah?" He replied, "There in the tent." [10A]One of them said, "I will surely return to you about this time next year, and Sarah will then have a son."

Responsorial Psalm: Psalms 15:2-3A, 3BC-4AB, 5

R. [(1a)] *He who does justice will live in the presence of the Lord.*

[2] One who walks blamelessly and does justice;
    who thinks the truth in his heart
[3A] and slanders not with his tongue.

R. *He who does justice will live in the presence of the Lord.*

[3BC] Who harms not his fellow man,
    nor takes up a reproach against his
        neighbor;
[4AB] by whom the reprobate is despised,
    while he honors those who fear the LORD.

R. *He who does justice will live in the presence of the Lord.*

[5] Who lends not his money at usury
    and accepts no bribe against the
        innocent.
One who does these things
    shall never be disturbed.

R. *He who does justice will live in the presence of the Lord.*

Second Reading: Colossians 1:24-28

Brothers and sisters: [4]Now I rejoice in my sufferings for your sake, and in my flesh I am filling up what is lacking in the afflictions of Christ on behalf of his body, which is the church, [25]of which I am a minister in accordance with God's stewardship given to me to bring to completion for you the word of God, [26]the mystery hidden from ages and from generations past. But now it has been manifested to his holy ones, [27]to whom God chose to make known the riches of the glory of this mystery among the Gentiles; it is Christ in you, the hope for glory. [28]It is he whom we proclaim, admonishing everyone and teaching everyone with all wisdom, that we may present everyone perfect in Christ.

Alleluia: cf. Luke 8:15

R. Alleluia, alleluia.
[15]Blessed are they who have kept the word
    with a generous heart
and yield a harvest through perseverance.

R. Alleluia, alleluia.

Gospel: Luke 10:38-42

[38]Jesus entered a village where a woman whose name was Martha welcomed him. [39]She had a sister named Mary who sat beside the Lord at his feet listening to him speak. [40]Martha, burdened with much serving, came to him and said, "Lord, do you not care that my sister has left me by myself to do the serving? Tell her to help me." [41]The Lord said to her in reply, "Martha, Martha, you are anxious and worried about many things. [42]There is need of only one thing. Mary has chosen the better part and it will not be taken from her."

Seventeenth Sunday in Ordinary Time, Year C

First Reading: Genesis 18:20-32

[20]In those days, the LORD said: "The outcry against Sodom and Gomorrah is so great, and their sin so grave, [21]that I must go down and see whether or not their actions fully correspond to the cry against them that comes to me. I mean to find out."

[22]While Abraham's visitors walked on farther toward Sodom, the LORD remained standing before Abraham. [23]Then Abraham drew nearer and said: "Will you sweep away the innocent with the guilty? [24]Suppose there were fifty innocent people in the city; would you wipe out the place, rather than spare it for the sake of the fifty innocent people within it?

[25] Far be it from you to do such a thing, to make the innocent die with the guilty so that the innocent and the guilty would be treated alike! Should not the judge of all the world act with justice?" [26]The LORD replied, "If I find fifty innocent people in the city of Sodom, I will spare the whole place for their sake." [27]Abraham spoke up again: "See how I am presuming to speak to my Lord, though I am but dust and ashes! [28]What if there are five less than fifty innocent people? Will you destroy the whole city because of those five?" He answered, "I will not destroy it, if I find forty-five there." [29]But Abraham persisted, saying "What if only forty are found there?" He replied, "I will forbear doing it for the sake of the forty." [30]Then Abraham said, "Let not my Lord grow impatient if I go on. What if only thirty are found there?" He replied, "I will forbear doing it if I can find but thirty there." [31]Still Abraham went on, "Since I have thus dared to speak to my Lord, what if there are no more than twenty?" The LORD answered, "I will not destroy it, for the sake of the twenty." [32]But he still persisted: "Please, let not my Lord grow angry if I speak up this last time. What if there are at least ten there?" He replied, "For the sake of those ten, I will not destroy it."

Responsorial Psalm: Psalms 138:1-2, 2-3, 6-7, 7-8

R. [3a] *Lord, on the day I called for help, you
answered me.*

[1]I will give thanks to you, O LORD, with all my
heart,
for you have heard the words of my

mouth;
    in the presence of the angels I will sing
        your praise;
2AB I will worship at your holy temple
    and give thanks to your name.

R. Lord, on the day I called for help, you
      answered me.

2BC Because of your kindness and your truth;
    for you have made great above all things
    your name and your promise.
3 When I called you answered me;
    you built up strength within me.

R. Lord, on the day I called for help, you
      answered me.

6 The LORD is exalted, yet the lowly he sees,
    and the proud he knows from afar.
7ABC Though I walk amid distress, you preserve
      me;
    against the anger of my enemies you
      raise your hand.

R. Lord, on the day I called for help, you
      answered me.

7C Your right hand saves me.
    8The LORD will complete what he has done
      for me;
your kindness, O LORD, endures forever;
    forsake not the work of your hands.

R. Lord, on the day I called for help, you
      answered me.

Second Reading: Colossians 2:12-14

Brothers and sisters: 12You were buried with him in baptism, in which you were also raised with him through faith in the power of God, who raised him from the dead. 13And even when you were dead in transgressions and the uncircumcision of your flesh, he brought you to life along with him, having forgiven us all our transgressions; 14obliterating the bond against us, with its legal claims, which was opposed to us, he also removed it from our midst, nailing it to the cross.

Alleluia: Romans 8:15BC

R. Alleluia, alleluia.
15BC You have received a Spirit of adoption,
through which we cry, Abba, Father.
R. Alleluia, alleluia.

Gospel: Luke 11:1-13

[1]Jesus was praying in a certain place, and when he had finished, one of his disciples said to him, "Lord, teach us to pray just as John taught his disciples." [2]He said to them, "When you pray, say:

Father, hallowed be your name,
> your kingdom come.
> [3]Give us each day our daily bread
> [4]and forgive us our sins
> for we ourselves forgive everyone in debt
> > to us,
> and do not subject us to the final test."

[5]And he said to them, "Suppose one of you has a friend to whom he goes at midnight and says, 'Friend, lend me three loaves of bread, [6]for a friend of mine has arrived at my house from a journey and I have nothing to offer him,' [7]and he says in reply from within, 'Do not bother me; the door has already been locked and my children and I are already in bed. I cannot get up to give you anything.' [8]I tell you, if he does not get up to give the visitor the loaves because of their friendship, he will get up to give him whatever he needs because of his persistence.

[9]"And I tell you, ask and you will receive; seek and you will find; knock and the door will be opened to you. [10] For everyone who asks, receives; and the one who seeks, finds; and to the one who knocks, the door will be opened. [11]What father among you would hand his son a snake when he asks for a fish? [12] Or hand him a scorpion when he asks for an egg? [13] If you then, who are wicked, know how to give good gifts to your children, how much more will the Father in heaven give the Holy Spirit to those who ask him?"

AUGUST 2025
Sunday August 3, 2025
Eighteenth Sunday in Ordinary Time, Year C
First Reading: Ecclesiastes 1:2; 2:21-23

[2]Vanity of vanities, says Qoheleth,
> vanity of vanities! All things are vanity!

[21]Here is one who has labored with wisdom and knowledge and skill, and yet to another who has not labored over it, he must leave property. This also is vanity and a great misfortune.

[22]For what profit comes to man from all the toil and anxiety of heart with which he has labored under the sun? [23]All his days sorrow and grief are his occupation; even at night his mind is not at rest. This also is vanity.

Responsorial Psalm: Psalms 90:3-4, 5-6, 12-13, 14 AND 17

R. [1] *If today you hear his voice, harden not your hearts.*

3 You turn man back to dust,
  saying, "Return, O children of men."
4 For a thousand years in your sight
  are as yesterday, now that it is past,
  or as a watch of the night.

R. *If today you hear his voice, harden not your hearts.*

5 You make an end of them in their sleep;
  the next morning they are like the
    changing grass,
6 Which at dawn springs up anew,
  but by evening wilts and fades.

R. *If today you hear his voice, harden not your hearts.*

12 Teach us to number our days aright,
  that we may gain wisdom of heart.
13 Return, O LORD! How long?
  Have pity on your servants!

R. *If today you hear his voice, harden not your hearts.*

14 Fill us at daybreak with your kindness,
  that we may shout for joy and gladness
    all our days.
17 And may the gracious care of the LORD our
    God be ours;
  prosper the work of our hands for us!
  Prosper the work of our hands!

R. *If today you hear his voice, harden not your hearts.*

Second Reading: Colossians 3:1-5, 9-11

Brothers and sisters: 1If you were raised with Christ, seek what is above, where Christ is seated at the right hand of God. 2Think of what is above, not of what is on earth. 3For you have died, and your life is hidden with Christ in God. 4When Christ your life appears, then you too will appear with him in glory.

5Put to death, then, the parts of you that are earthly: immorality, impurity, passion, evil desire, and the greed that is idolatry. 9Stop lying to one another, since you have taken off the old self with its practices 10and have put on the new self, which is being renewed, for knowledge, in the image of its creator. 11Here there is not Greek and Jew, circumcision and uncircumcision, barbarian, Scythian, slave, free; but Christ is all and in all.

Alleluia: Matthew 5:3

R. Alleluia, alleluia.
[3] Blessed are the poor in spirit,
for theirs is the kingdom of heaven.
R. Alleluia, alleluia.

Gospel: Luke 12:13-21

[13]Someone in the crowd said to Jesus, "Teacher, tell my brother to share the inheritance with me." [14]He replied to him, "Friend, who appointed me as your judge and arbitrator?" [15]Then he said to the crowd, "Take care to guard against all greed, for though one may be rich, one's life does not consist of possessions."

[16]Then he told them a parable. "There was a rich man whose land produced a bountiful harvest. [17]He asked himself, 'What shall I do, for I do not have space to store my harvest?' [18]And he said, 'This is what I shall do: I shall tear down my barns and build larger ones. There I shall store all my grain and other goods [19]and I shall say to myself, "Now as for you, you have so many good things stored up for many years, rest, eat, drink, be merry!"' [20]But God said to him, 'You fool, this night your life will be demanded of you; and the things you have prepared, to whom will they belong?' [21]Thus will it be for all who store up treasure for themselves but are not rich in what matters to God."

Sunday August 10, 2025
Nineteenth Sunday in Ordinary Time, Year C
First Reading: Wisdom 18:6-9

[6]The night of the passover was known
        beforehand to our fathers,
    that, with sure knowledge of the oaths in
        which they put their faith,
    they might have courage.
[7]Your people awaited the salvation of the just
    and the destruction of their foes.
[8]For when you punished our adversaries,
    in this you glorified us whom you had
        summoned.
[9]For in secret the holy children of the good
        were offering sacrifice
    and putting into effect with one accord
        the divine institution.

Responsorial Psalm: Psalms 33:1, 12, 18-19, 20-22

R. [12b] *Blessed the people the Lord has chosen*
        to be his own.
[1] Exult, you just, in the LORD;

praise from the upright is fitting.
¹² Blessed the nation whose God is the LORD,
 the people he has chosen for his own
  inheritance.

R. Blessed the people the Lord has chosen to be
  his own.

¹⁸ See, the eyes of the LORD are upon those who
  fear him,
 upon those who hope for his kindness,
¹⁹ To deliver them from death
 and preserve them in spite of famine.

R. Blessed the people the Lord has chosen to be
  his own.

²⁰ Our soul waits for the LORD,
 who is our help and our shield.
²² May your kindness, O LORD, be upon us
 who have put our hope in you.

R. Blessed the people the Lord has chosen to be
  his own.

Second Reading: Hebrews 11:1-2, 8-19

Brothers and sisters: ¹Faith is the realization of what is hoped for and evidence of things not seen. ²Because of it the ancients were well attested.

⁸By faith Abraham obeyed when he was called to go out to a place that he was to receive as an inheritance; he went out, not knowing where he was to go. ⁹By faith he sojourned in the promised land as in a foreign country, dwelling in tents with Isaac and Jacob, heirs of the same promise; ¹⁰for he was looking forward to the city with foundations, whose architect and maker is God. ¹¹By faith he received power to generate, even though he was past the normal age —and Sarah herself was sterile— for he thought that the one who had made the promise was trustworthy. ¹²So it was that there came forth from one man, himself as good as dead, descendants as numerous as the stars in the sky and as countless as the sands on the seashore.

¹³All these died in faith. They did not receive what had been promised but saw it and greeted it from afar and acknowledged themselves to be strangers and aliens on earth, ¹⁴for those who speak thus show that they are seeking a homeland. ¹⁵If they had been thinking of the land from which they had come, they would have had opportunity to return. ¹⁶But now they desire a better homeland, a heavenly one. Therefore, God is not ashamed to be called their God, for he has prepared a city for them.

¹⁷By faith Abraham, when put to the test, offered up Isaac, and he who had received the promises was ready to offer his only son, ¹⁸of whom it was said, "Through Isaac descendants shall bear your name." He reasoned that God was able to raise even from the dead, and he received Isaac back as a symbol.

Or Hebrews 11:1-2, 8-12

Brothers and sisters: [1]Faith is the realization of what is hoped for and evidence of things not seen. [2]Because of it the ancients were well attested.

[8]By faith Abraham obeyed when he was called to go out to a place that he was to receive as an inheritance; he went out, not knowing where he was to go. [9]By faith he sojourned in the promised land as in a foreign country, dwelling in tents with Isaac and Jacob, heirs of the same promise; [10]for he was looking forward to the city with foundations, whose architect and maker is God. [11]By faith he received power to generate, even though he was past the normal age —and Sarah herself was sterile— for he thought that the one who had made the promise was trustworthy. [12]So it was that there came forth from one man, himself as good as dead, descendants as numerous as the stars in the sky and as countless as the sands on the seashore.

Alleluia: Matthew 24;42A, 44

R. Alleluia, alleluia.
[42A] Stay awake and be ready!
[44] For you do not know on what day your
       Lord will come.
R. Alleluia, alleluia.

Gospel: Luke 12:32-48

Jesus said to his disciples: [32]"Do not be afraid any longer, little flock, for your Father is pleased to give you the kingdom. [33]Sell your belongings and give alms. Provide money bags for yourselves that do not wear out, an inexhaustible treasure in heaven that no thief can reach nor moth destroy. [34]For where your treasure is, there also will your heart be.

[35]"Gird your loins and light your lamps [36]and be like servants who await their master's return from a wedding, ready to open immediately when he comes and knocks. [37]Blessed are those servants whom the master finds vigilant on his arrival. Amen, I say to you, he will gird himself, have them recline at table, and proceed to wait on them. [38]And should he come in the second or third watch and find them prepared in this way, blessed are those servants. [39]Be sure of this: if the master of the house had known the hour when the thief was coming, he would not have let his house be broken into. [40]You also must be prepared, for at an hour you do not expect, the Son of Man will come." [41]Then Peter said, "Lord, is this parable meant for us or for everyone?" [42]And the Lord replied, "Who, then, is the faithful and prudent steward whom the master will put in charge of his servants to distribute the food allowance at the proper time? [43]Blessed is that servant whom his master on arrival finds doing so. [44]Truly, I say to you, the master will put the servant in charge of all his property. [45]But if that servant says to himself, 'My master is delayed in coming,' and begins to beat the menservants and the maidservants, to eat and drink and get drunk, [46]then that servant's master will

come on an unexpected day and at an unknown hour and will punish the servant severely and assign him a place with the unfaithful. [47]That servant who knew his master's will but did not make preparations nor act in accord with his will shall be beaten severely; [48]and the servant who was ignorant of his master's will but acted in a way deserving of a severe beating shall be beaten only lightly. Much will be required of the person entrusted with much, and still more will be demanded of the person entrusted with more."

Or Luke 12:35-40

Jesus said to his disciples: [35]"Gird your loins and light your lamps [36]and be like servants who await their master's return from a wedding, ready to open immediately when he comes and knocks. [37]Blessed are those servants whom the master finds vigilant on his arrival. Amen, I say to you, he will gird himself, have them recline at table, and proceed to wait on them. [38]And should he come in the second or third watch and find them prepared in this way, blessed are those servants. [39]Be sure of this: if the master of the house had known the hour when the thief was coming, he would not have let his house be broken into. [40]You also must be prepared, for at an hour you do not expect, the Son of Man will come."

Sunday August 17, 2025
Twentieth Sunday in Ordinary Time, Year C
First Reading: Jeremiah 38:4-6, 8-10

[4]In those days, the princes said to the king: "Jeremiah ought to be put to death; he is demoralizing the soldiers who are left in this city, and all the people, by speaking such things to them; he is not interested in the welfare of our people, but in their ruin." [5]King Zedekiah answered: "He is in your power"; for the king could do nothing with them. [6]And so they took Jeremiah and threw him into the cistern of Prince Malchiah, which was in the quarters of the guard, letting him down with ropes. There was no water in the cistern, only mud, and Jeremiah sank into the mud.

[8]Ebed-melech, a court official, went there from the palace and said to him: [9]"My lord king, these men have been at fault in all they have done to the prophet Jeremiah, casting him into the cistern. He will die of famine on the spot, for there is no more food in the city." [10]Then the king ordered Ebed-melech the Cushite to take three men along with him, and draw the prophet Jeremiah out of the cistern before he should die.

Responsorial Psalm: Psalms 40:2, 3, 4, 18

R. [14b] *Lord, come to my aid!*
[2]I have waited, waited for the LORD,
　　and he stooped toward me.
R. Lord, come to my aid!
[3]The LORD heard my cry.
He drew me out of the pit of destruction,
　　out of the mud of the swamp;
he set my feet upon a crag;
　　he made firm my steps.

R. Lord, come to my aid!
[4]And he put a new song into my mouth,
        a hymn to our God.
Many shall look on in awe
        and trust in the LORD.
R. Lord, come to my aid!
[18] Though I am afflicted and poor,
        yet the LORD thinks of me.
You are my help and my deliverer;
        O my God, hold not back!
R. Lord, come to my aid!

Second Reading: Hebrews 12:1-4

Brothers and sisters: [1]Since we are surrounded by so great a cloud of witnesses, let us rid ourselves of every burden and sin that clings to us and persevere in running the race that lies before us [2]while keeping our eyes fixed on Jesus, the leader and perfecter of faith. For the sake of the joy that lay before him he endured the cross, despising its shame, and has taken his seat at the right of the throne of God. [3]Consider how he endured such opposition from sinners, in order that you may not grow weary and lose heart. [4]In your struggle against sin you have not yet resisted to the point of shedding blood.

Alleluia: John 10:27

R. Alleluia, alleluia.
[27]My sheep hear my voice, says the Lord;
I know them, and they follow me.
R. Alleluia, alleluia.

Gospel: Luke 12:49-53

Jesus said to his disciples: [49]"I have come to set the earth on fire, and how I wish it were already blazing!
[50]There is a baptism with which I must be baptized, and how great is my anguish until it is accomplished! [51]Do you think that I have come to establish peace on the earth? No, I tell you, but rather division. [52]From now on a household of five will be divided, three against two and two against three; [53]a father will be divided against his son and a son against his father, a mother against her daughter and a daughter against her mother, a mother-in-law against her daughter-in-law and a daughter-in-law against her mother-in-law."

Sunday August 24, 2025

Twenty-first Sunday in Ordinary Time, Year C

First Reading: Isaiah 66:18-21

[18] Thus says the LORD:

I know their works and their thoughts,
and I come to gather nations of every
        language;
    they shall come and see my glory.
¹⁹I will set a sign among them;
    from them I will send fugitives to the
        nations:
    to Tarshish, Put and Lud, Mosoch, Tubal
        and Javan,
    to the distant coastlands
    that have never heard of my fame, or
        seen my glory;
    and they shall proclaim my glory among
        the nations.
²⁰ They shall bring all your brothers and sisters
        from all the nations
    as an offering to the LORD,
    on horses and in chariots, in carts, upon
        mules and dromedaries,
    to Jerusalem, my holy mountain, says the
        LORD,
    just as the Israelites bring their offering
    to the house of the LORD in clean vessels.
²¹ Some of these I will take as priests and
        Levites, says the LORD.

Responsorial Psalm: Psalms 117:1, 2

R. *(Mk 16:15)* **Go out to all the world and tell the
            Good News.** or: **R. Alleluia**.
¹ Praise the LORD all you nations;
        glorify him, all you peoples!
**R. Go out to all the world and tell the Good
            News.** or: **R. Alleluia**.
² For steadfast is his kindness toward us,
        and the fidelity of the LORD endures
            forever.
**R. Go out to all the world and tell the Good
            News.** or: **R. Alleluia**.

Second Reading: Hebrews 12:5-7, 11-13

Brothers and sisters, ⁵You have forgotten the exhortation addressed to you as
children:

"My son, do not disdain the discipline of the

Lord
or lose heart when reproved by him;
[6]for whom the Lord loves, he disciplines;
he scourges every son he acknowledges."

[7]Endure your trials as "discipline"; God treats you as sons. For what "son" is there whom his father does not discipline? [11]At the time, all discipline seems a cause not for joy but for pain, yet later it brings the peaceful fruit of righteousness to those who are trained by it.

[12]So strengthen your drooping hands and your weak knees. [13]Make straight paths for your feet, that what is lame may not be disjointed but healed.

Alleluia: John 14:6
R. Alleluia, alleluia.
[6] I am the way, the truth and the life, says the
Lord;
no one comes to the Father, except through
me.
R. Alleluia, alleluia.

Gospel: Luke 13:22-30
[22]Jesus passed through towns and villages, teaching as he went and making his way to Jerusalem. [23]Someone asked him, "Lord, will only a few people be saved?" He answered them, [24]"Strive to enter through the narrow gate, for many, I tell you, will attempt to enter but will not be strong enough. [25]After the master of the house has arisen and locked the door, then will you stand outside knocking and saying, 'Lord, open the door for us.' He will say to you in reply, 'I do not know where you are from. [26]And you will say, 'We ate and drank in your company and you taught in our streets.' [27]Then he will say to you, 'I do not know where you are from. Depart from me, all you evildoers!' [28]And there will be wailing and grinding of teeth when you see Abraham, Isaac, and Jacob and all the prophets in the kingdom of God and you yourselves cast out. [29]And people will come from the east and the west and from the north and the south and will recline at table in the kingdom of God. [30]For behold, some are last who will be first, and some are first who will be last."

Sunday August 31, 2025
Twenty-second Sunday in ordinary Time, Year C
First Reading: Sirach 3:17-18, 21, 29-30
[17]My child, conduct your affairs with humility,
and you will be loved more than a giver
of gifts.
[18]Humble yourself the more, the greater you
are,
and you will find favor with God.
[21]What is too sublime for you, seek not,

into things beyond your strength search
  not.
29 The mind of a sage appreciates proverbs,
  and an attentive ear is the joy of the wise.
30 Water quenches a flaming fire,
  and alms atone for sins.

Responsorial Psalm: Psalms 68:4-5, 6-7, 10-11

R. *(cf. 11b)* ***God, in your goodness, you have made***
    a home for the poor.

4The just rejoice and exult before God;
  they are glad and rejoice.
5Sing to God, chant praise to his name,
  whose name is the LORD.

R. God, in your goodness, you have made a
   home for the poor.

6 The father of orphans and the defender of
   widows
  is God in his holy dwelling.
7 God gives a home to the forsaken;
  he leads forth prisoners to prosperity.

R. God, in your goodness, you have made a
   home for the poor.

10 A bountiful rain you showered down, O God,
   upon your inheritance;
  you restored the land when it languished;
11 your flock settled in it;
  in your goodness, O God, you provided it
   for the needy.

R. God, in your goodness, you have made a
   home for the poor.

Second Reading: Hebrews 12:18-19, 22-24A

Brothers and sisters: 18You have not approached that which could be touched and a blazing fire and gloomy darkness 19and storm and a trumpet blast and a voice speaking words such that those who heard begged that no message be further addressed to them. 22No, you have approached Mount Zion and the city of the living God, the heavenly Jerusalem, and countless angels in festal gathering, 23and the assembly of the firstborn enrolled in heaven, and God the judge of all, and the spirits of the just made perfect, 24and Jesus, the mediator of a new covenant, and the sprinkled blood that speaks more eloquently than that of Abel.

Alleluia: Matthew 11:29AB

R. Alleluia, alleluia.

²⁹Take my yoke upon you, says the Lord,
and learn from me, for I am meek and
    humble of heart.
R. Alleluia, alleluia.

Gospel: Luke 14:1, 7-14

¹On a sabbath Jesus went to dine at the home of one of the leading Pharisees, and the people there were observing him carefully.

⁷He told a parable to those who had been invited, noticing how they were choosing the places of honor at the table. ⁸"When you are invited by someone to a wedding banquet, do not recline at table in the place of honor. A more distinguished guest than you may have been invited by him, ⁹and the host who invited both of you may approach you and say, 'Give your place to this man,' and then you would proceed with embarrassment to take the lowest place. ¹⁰Rather, when you are invited, go and take the lowest place so that when the host comes to you he may say, 'My friend, move up to a higher position.' Then you will enjoy the esteem of your companions at the table. ¹¹For everyone who exalts himself will be humbled, but the one who humbles himself will be exalted." ¹²Then he said to the host who invited him, "When you hold a lunch or a dinner, do not invite your friends or your brothers or your relatives or your wealthy neighbors, in case they may invite you back and you have repayment.

¹³ Rather, when you hold a banquet, invite the poor, the crippled, the lame, the blind; ¹⁴Blessed indeed will you be because of their inability to repay you. For you will be repaid at the resurrection of the righteous."

SEPTEMBER 2025
Sunday September 7, 2025
Twenty-third Sunday in Ordinary Time, Year C

First Reading: Wisdom 9:13-18B

¹³Who can know God's counsel,
    or who can conceive what the LORD
        intends?
¹⁴For the deliberations of mortals are timid,
    and unsure are our plans.
¹⁵For the corruptible body burdens the soul
    and the earthen shelter weighs down the
        mind that has many concerns.
¹⁶ And scarce do we guess the things on earth,
    and what is within our grasp we find

with difficulty;
    but when things are in heaven, who can
        search them out?
[17] Or who ever knew your counsel, except you
        had given wisdom
    and sent your holy spirit from on high?
[18B] And thus were the paths of those on earth
        made straight.

Responsorial Psalm: Psalms 90:3-4, 5-6, 12-13, 14 AND 17

R. [1] *In every age, O Lord, you have been our*
        refuge.
[3] You turn man back to dust,
    saying, "Return, O children of men."
[4] For a thousand years in your sight
    are as yesterday, now that it is past,
    or as a watch of the night.

R. In every age, O Lord, you have been our
        refuge.
[5] You make an end of them in their sleep;
    the next morning they are like the
        changing grass,
[6] Which at dawn springs up anew,
    but by evening wilts and fades.

R. In every age, O Lord, you have been our
        refuge.
[12] Teach us to number our days aright,
    that we may gain wisdom of heart.
[13] Return, O LORD! How long?
    Have pity on your servants!

R. In every age, O Lord, you have been our
        refuge.
[14] Fill us at daybreak with your kindness,
    that we may shout for joy and gladness
        all our days.
[17] And may the gracious care of the LORD our
        God be ours;
    prosper the work of our hands for us!
    Prosper the work of our hands!

R. In every age, O Lord, you have been our
        refuge.

Second Reading: Philemon 9-10, 12-17

⁹I, Paul, an old man, and now also a prisoner for Christ Jesus, ¹⁰urge you on behalf of my child Onesimus, whose father I have become in my imprisonment; ¹²I am sending him, that is, my own heart, back to you. ¹³I should have liked to retain him for myself, so that he might serve me on your behalf in my imprisonment for the gospel, ¹⁴but I did not want to do anything without your consent, so that the good you do might not be forced but voluntary. ¹⁵Perhaps this is why he was away from you for a while, that you might have him back forever, ¹⁶no longer as a slave but more than a slave, a brother, beloved especially to me, but even more so to you, as a man and in the Lord. ¹⁷So if you regard me as a partner, welcome him as you would me.

Alleluia: Psalms 119:135
R. Alleluia, alleluia.
¹³⁵ Let your face shine upon your servant;
and teach me your laws.
R. Alleluia, alleluia.

Gospel: Luke 14:25-33
²⁵Great crowds were traveling with Jesus, and he turned and addressed them, ²⁶"If anyone comes to me without hating his father and mother, wife and children, brothers and sisters, and even his own life, he cannot be my disciple. ²⁷Whoever does not carry his own cross and come after me cannot be my disciple. ²⁸Which of you wishing to construct a tower does not first sit down and calculate the cost to see if there is enough for its completion? ²⁹Otherwise, after laying the foundation and finding himself unable to finish the work the onlookers should laugh at him ³⁰and say, 'This one began to build but did not have the resources to finish.' ³¹Or what king marching into battle would not first sit down and decide whether with ten thousand troops he can successfully oppose another king advancing upon him with twenty thousand troops? ³²But if not, while he is still far away, he will send a delegation to ask for peace terms. ³³In the same way, anyone of you who does not renounce all his possessions cannot be my disciple."

Sunday September 14, 2025
Feast of the Exaltation of the Holy Cross
First Reading: Numbers 21:4B-9
^{4B} With their patience worn out by the journey, ⁵ the people complained against God and Moses, "Why have you brought us up from Egypt to die in this desert, where there is no food or water? We are disgusted with this wretched food!"

⁶ In punishment the LORD sent among the people saraph serpents, which bit the people so that many of them died. ⁷ Then the people came to Moses and said, "We have sinned in complaining against the LORD and you. Pray the LORD to take the serpents from us." So Moses prayed for the people, ⁸ and the LORD said to Moses, "Make a saraph and mount it on a pole, and if any who have been bitten look at it, they will live." ⁹ Moses accordingly made a bronze serpent and

mounted it on a pole, and whenever anyone who had been bitten by a serpent looked at the bronze serpent, he lived.

Responsorial Psalm: Psalms 78:1BC-2, 34-35, 36-37, 38

R. *(See 7b)* **Do not forget the works of the Lord!**

1BC Hearken, my people, to my teaching;
    incline your ears to the words of my
        mouth.
2 I will open my mouth in a parable,
    I will utter mysteries from of old.

R. Do not forget the works of the Lord!

34 While he slew them they sought him
    and inquired after God again,
35 Remembering that God was their rock
    and the Most High God, their redeemer.

R. Do not forget the works of the Lord!

36 But they flattered him with their mouths
    and lied to him with their tongues,
37 Though their hearts were not steadfast
      toward him,
    nor were they faithful to his covenant.

R. Do not forget the works of the Lord!

38 But he, being merciful, forgave their sin
    and destroyed them not;
Often he turned back his anger
    and let none of his wrath be roused.

R. Do not forget the works of the Lord!

Second Reading: Philippians 2:6-11

Brothers and sisters:

6 Christ Jesus, though he was in the form of
      God,
    did not regard equality with God
    something to be grasped.
7 Rather, he emptied himself,
    taking the form of a slave,
    coming in human likeness;
    and found human in appearance,
8 he humbled himself,
    becoming obedient to death,
    even death on a cross.
9 Because of this, God greatly exalted him
    and bestowed on him the name

that is above every name,
¹⁰ that at the name of Jesus
every knee should bend,
of those in heaven and on earth and
        under the earth,
¹¹ and every tongue confess that
Jesus Christ is Lord,
to the glory of God the Father.

Alleluia
R. Alleluia, alleluia.
We adore you, O Christ, and we bless you,
because by your Cross you have redeemed
        the world.
R. Alleluia, alleluia.

Gospel: John 3:13-17
Jesus said to Nicodemus: ¹³ "No one has gone up to heaven except the one who has come down from heaven, the Son of Man. ¹⁴ And just as Moses lifted up the serpent in the desert, so must the Son of Man be lifted up, ¹⁵ so that everyone who believes in him may have eternal life."

¹⁶ For God so loved the world that he gave his only Son, so that everyone who believes in him might not perish but might have eternal life. ¹⁷ For God did not send his Son into the world to condemn the world, but that the world might be saved through him.

Twenty-fifth Sunday in Ordinary Time, Year C
First Reading: Amos 8:4-7
⁴Hear this, you who trample upon the needy
        and destroy the poor of the land!
⁵"When will the new moon be over," you ask,
        "that we may sell our grain,
        and the sabbath, that we may display the
                wheat?
We will diminish the ephah,
        add to the shekel,
        and fix our scales for cheating!
⁶We will buy the lowly for silver,
        and the poor for a pair of sandals;
        even the refuse of the wheat we will sell!"
⁷The LORD has sworn by the pride of Jacob:
        Never will I forget a thing they have
                done!

Responsorial Psalm: Psalms 113:1-2, 4-6, 7-8

R. *(cf. 1a, 7b)* ***Praise the Lord who lifts up the poor.*** or: ***R. Alleluia.***

¹ Praise, you servants of the LORD,
    praise the name of the LORD.
² Blessed be the name of the LORD
    both now and forever.

R. Praise the Lord who lifts up the poor. or: ***R. Alleluia.***

⁴High above all nations is the LORD;
    above the heavens is his glory.
⁶ Who is like the LORD, our God, who is
        enthroned on high
    and looks upon the heavens and the earth
        below?

R. Praise the Lord who lifts up the poor. or: ***R. Alleluia.***

⁷ He raises up the lowly from the dust;
    from the dunghill he lifts up the poor
⁸ to seat them with princes,
    with the princes of his own people.

R. Praise the Lord who lifts up the poor. or: ***R. Alleluia.***

Second Reading: 1 Timothy 2:1-8

Beloved: ¹First of all, I ask that supplications, prayers, petitions, and thanksgivings be offered for everyone, ²for kings and for all in authority, that we may lead a quiet and tranquil life in all devotion and dignity. ³This is good and pleasing to God our savior, ⁴who wills everyone to be saved and to come to knowledge of the truth.

⁵For there is one God.
    There is also one mediator between God
        and men,
the man Christ Jesus,
    ⁶who gave himself as ransom for all.

This was the testimony at the proper time. ⁷For this I was appointed preacher and apostle —I am speaking the truth, I am not lying—, teacher of the Gentiles in faith and truth.
    ⁸It is my wish, then, that in every place the men should pray, lifting up holy hands, without anger or argument.

Alleluia: cf. 2 Corinthians 8:9

R. Alleluia, alleluia.
⁹Though our Lord Jesus Christ was rich, he
    became poor,
so that by his poverty you might become
    rich.

R. Alleluia, alleluia.

Gospel: Luke 16:1-13

[1]Jesus said to his disciples, "A rich man had a steward who was reported to him for squandering his property. [2]He summoned him and said, 'What is this I hear about you? Prepare a full account of your stewardship, because you can no longer be my steward.' [3]The steward said to himself, 'What shall I do, now that my master is taking the position of steward away from me? I am not strong enough to dig and I am ashamed to beg. [4]I know what I shall do so that, when I am removed from the stewardship, they may welcome me into their homes.' [5]He called in his master's debtors one by one. To the first he said, 'How much do you owe my master?' [6]He replied, 'One hundred measures of olive oil.' He said to him, 'Here is your promissory note. Sit down and quickly write one for fifty.' [7]Then to another the steward said, 'And you, how much do you owe?' He replied, 'One hundred kors of wheat.' The steward said to him, 'Here is your promissory note; write one for eighty.' [8]And the master commended that dishonest steward for acting prudently.

"For the children of this world are more prudent in dealing with their own generation than are the children of light. [9]I tell you, make friends for yourselves with dishonest wealth, so that when it fails, you will be welcomed into eternal dwellings. [10]The person who is trustworthy in very small matters is also trustworthy in great ones; and the person who is dishonest in very small matters is also dishonest in great ones. [11]If, therefore, you are not trustworthy with dishonest wealth, who will trust you with true wealth? [12]If you are not trustworthy with what belongs to another, who will give you what is yours? [13]No servant can serve two masters. He will either hate one and love the other, or be devoted to one and despise the other. You cannot serve both God and mammon."

Or Luke 16:10-13

Jesus said to his disciples: [10]The person who is trustworthy in very small matters is also trustworthy in great ones; and the person who is dishonest in very small matters is also dishonest in great ones. [11]If, therefore, you are not trustworthy with dishonest wealth, who will trust you with true wealth? [12]If you are not trustworthy with what belongs to another, who will give you what is yours? [13]No servant can serve two masters. He will either hate one and love the other, or be devoted to one and despise the other. You cannot serve both God and mammon."

Sunday September 28, 2025
Twenty-sixth Sunday in Ordinary Time, Year C
First Reading: Amos 6:1A, 4-7

Thus says the LORD, the God of hosts:

[1A]Woe to the complacent in Zion!
[4]Lying upon beds of ivory,
    stretched comfortably on their couches,
they eat lambs taken from the flock,

and calves from the stall!
5Improvising to the music of the harp,
    like David, they devise their own
        accompaniment.
6They drink wine from bowls
    and anoint themselves with the best oils;
    yet they are not made ill by the collapse
        of Joseph!
7Therefore, now they shall be the first to go
        into exile,
and their wanton revelry shall be done
        away with.

Responsorial Psalm: Psalms 146:7, 8-9, 9-10

R. (1b) *Praise the Lord, my soul!* or: R. *Alleluia.*
7Blessed he who keeps faith forever,
    secures justice for the oppressed,
    gives food to the hungry.
The LORD sets captives free.
R. *Praise the Lord, my soul!* or: R. *Alleluia.*
8The LORD gives sight to the blind;
    the LORD raises up those who were bowed
        down.
The LORD loves the just;
    9A the LORD protects strangers.
R. *Praise the Lord, my soul!* or: R. *Alleluia.*
9B The fatherless and the widow he sustains,
    but the way of the wicked he thwarts.
10 The LORD shall reign forever;
    your God, O Zion, through all
        generations. Alleluia.
R. *Praise the Lord, my soul!* or: R. *Alleluia.*

Second Reading: 1 Timothy 6:11-16

11But you, man of God, pursue righteousness, devotion, faith, love, patience, and gentleness. 12Compete well for the faith. Lay hold of eternal life, to which you were called when you made the noble confession in the presence of many witnesses. 13I charge you before God, who gives life to all things, and before Christ Jesus, who gave testimony under Pontius Pilate for the noble confession, 14to keep the commandment without stain or reproach until the appearance of our Lord Jesus Christ 15that the blessed and only ruler will make manifest at the proper time, the King of kings and Lord of lords, 16who alone has immortality, who dwells in unapproachable light, and whom no human being has seen or can see. To him be honor and eternal power. Amen.

Alleluia: 2 Corinthians 8:9

R. Alleluia, alleluia.

[9]Though our Lord Jesus Christ was rich, he
became poor,
so that by his poverty you might become
rich.

R. Alleluia, alleluia.

Gospel: Luke 16:19-31

Jesus said to the Pharisees: [19]"There was a rich man who dressed in purple garments and fine linen and dined sumptuously each day. [20]And lying at his door was a poor man named Lazarus, covered with sores, [21]who would gladly have eaten his fill of the scraps that fell from the rich man's table. Dogs even used to come and lick his sores. [22]When the poor man died, he was carried away by angels to the bosom of Abraham. The rich man also died and was buried, [23]and from the netherworld, where he was in torment, he raised his eyes and saw Abraham far off and Lazarus at his side. [24]And he cried out, 'Father Abraham, have pity on me. Send Lazarus to dip the tip of his finger in water and cool my tongue, for I am suffering torment in these flames.' [25]Abraham replied, 'My child, remember that you received what was good during your lifetime while Lazarus likewise received what was bad; but now he is comforted here, whereas you are tormented. [26]Moreover, between us and you a great chasm is established to prevent anyone from crossing who might wish to go from our side to yours or from your side to ours.' [27]He said, 'Then I beg you, father, send him to my father's house, [28]for I have five brothers, so that he may warn them, lest they too come to this place of torment.' [29]But Abraham replied, 'They have Moses and the prophets. Let them listen to them.' [30]He said, 'Oh no, father Abraham, but if someone from the dead goes to them, they will repent.' [31]Then Abraham said, 'If they will not listen to Moses and the prophets, neither will they be persuaded if someone should rise from the dead.'"

OCTOBER 2025
Sunday October 5, 2025
Twenty-seventh Sunday in Ordinary Time, Year C
First Reading: Habakkuk 1:2-3; 2:2-4

[2]How long, O LORD? I cry for help
but you do not listen!
I cry out to you, "Violence!"
but you do not intervene.
[3]Why do you let me see ruin;
why must I look at misery?
Destruction and violence are before me;

there is strife, and clamorous discord.
²Then the LORD answered me and said:
>Write down the vision clearly upon the
>tablets,
>so that one can read it readily.
³For the vision still has its time,
>presses on to fulfillment, and will not
>disappoint;
if it delays, wait for it,
>it will surely come, it will not be late.
⁴The rash one has no integrity;
>but the just one, because of his faith, shall
>live.

Responsorial Psalm: Psalms 95:1-2, 6-7, 8-9

R. *(8)* *If today you hear his voice, harden not your hearts.*

¹ Come, let us sing joyfully to the LORD;
>let us acclaim the Rock of our salvation.
² Let us come into his presence with
>thanksgiving;
>let us joyfully sing psalms to him.

R. *If today you hear his voice, harden not your hearts.*

⁶ Come, let us bow down in worship;
>let us kneel before the LORD who made us.
⁷ For he is our God,
>and we are the people he shepherds, the
>flock he guides.

R. *If today you hear his voice, harden not your hearts.*

⁸ Oh, that today you would hear his voice:
>"Harden not your hearts as at Meribah,
>as in the day of Massah in the desert,
⁹ Where your fathers tempted me;
>they tested me though they had seen my
>works."

R. *If today you hear his voice, harden not your hearts.*

Second Reading: 2 Timothy 1:6-8, 13-14

Beloved: ⁶I remind you, to stir into flame the gift of God that you have through the imposition of my hands. ⁷For God did not give us a spirit of cowardice but rather of power and love and self-control. ⁸So do not be ashamed of your testimony to our Lord, nor of me, a prisoner for his sake; but bear your share of hardship for the gospel with the strength that comes from God.

¹³Take as your norm the sound words that you heard from me, in the faith and love that are in Christ Jesus. ¹⁴Guard this rich trust with the help of the Holy Spirit that dwells within us.

Alleluia: 1 Peter 1:25
R. Alleluia, alleluia.
²⁵The word of the Lord remains for ever.
This is the word that has been proclaimed to you.
R. Alleluia, alleluia.

Gospel: Luke 17:5-10
⁵The apostles said to the Lord, "Increase our faith." ⁶The Lord replied, "If you have faith the size of a mustard seed, you would say to this mulberry tree, 'Be uprooted and planted in the sea,' and it would obey you.

⁷"Who among you would say to your servant who has just come in from plowing or tending sheep in the field, 'Come here immediately and take your place at table'? ⁸Would he not rather say to him, 'Prepare something for me to eat. Put on your apron and wait on me while I eat and drink. You may eat and drink when I am finished'? ⁹Is he grateful to that servant because he did what was commanded? ¹⁰So should it be with you. When you have done all you have been commanded, say, 'We are unprofitable servants; we have done what we were obliged to do.'"

Sunday October 12, 2025
Twenty-eighth Sunday in Ordinary Time, Year C
First Reading: 2 Kings 5:14-17
¹⁴Naaman went down and plunged into the Jordan seven times at the word of Elisha, the man of God. His flesh became again like the flesh of a little child, and he was clean of his leprosy.

¹⁵Naaman returned with his whole retinue to the man of God. On his arrival he stood before Elisha and said, "Now I know that there is no God in all the earth, except in Israel. Please accept a gift from your servant."

¹⁶Elisha replied, "As the LORD lives whom I serve, I will not take it;" and despite Naaman's urging, he still refused. ¹⁷Naaman said: "If you will not accept, please let me, your servant, have two mule-loads of earth, for I will no longer offer holocaust or sacrifice to any other god except to the LORD."

Responsorial Psalm: Psalms 98:1, 2-3, 3-4
R. (cf. 2b) **The Lord has revealed to the nations his**
        saving power.
¹Sing to the LORD a new song,
    for he has done wondrous deeds;

110

his right hand has won victory for him,
    his holy arm.
R. The Lord has revealed to the nations his
       saving power.
[2] The LORD has made his salvation known:
    in the sight of the nations he has revealed
      his justice.
[3AB] He has remembered his kindness and his
    faithfulness
    toward the house of Israel.
R. The Lord has revealed to the nations his
       saving power.
[3CD] All the ends of the earth have seen
    the salvation by our God.
[4] Sing joyfully to the LORD, all you lands:
    break into song; sing praise.
R. The Lord has revealed to the nations his
       saving power.

Second Reading: 2 Timothy 2:8-13

Beloved: [8]Remember Jesus Christ, raised from the dead, a descendant of David: such is my gospel, [9]for which I am suffering, even to the point of chains, like a criminal. But the word of God is not chained. [10]Therefore, I bear with everything for the sake of those who are chosen, so that they too may obtain the salvation that is in Christ Jesus, together with eternal glory. [11]This saying is trustworthy:

If we have died with him
    we shall also live with him;
[12]if we persevere
    we shall also reign with him.
But if we deny him
    he will deny us.
[13]If we are unfaithful
    he remains faithful,
    for he cannot deny himself.

Alleluia: 1 Thessalonians 5:18
R. Alleluia, alleluia.
[18] In all circumstances, give thanks,
for this is the will of God for you in Christ
    Jesus.
R. Alleluia, alleluia.

Gospel: Luke 17:11-19

[11]As Jesus continued his journey to Jerusalem, he traveled through Samaria and Galilee. [12]As he was entering a village, ten lepers met him. They stood at a distance from him [13]and raised their voices, saying, "Jesus, Master! Have pity on us!" [14]And when he saw them, he said, "Go show yourselves to the priests." As they were going they were cleansed. [15]And one of them, realizing he had been healed, returned, glorifying God in a loud voice; [16]and he fell at the feet of Jesus and thanked him. He was a Samaritan.[17]Jesus said in reply, "Ten were cleansed, were they not? Where are the other nine? [18]Has none but this foreigner returned to give thanks to God?" [19]Then he said to him, "Stand up and go; your faith has saved you."

Sunday October 19, 2025
Twenty-ninth Week Sunday in Ordinary Time, Year C
First Reading: Exodus 17:8-13

[8]In those days, Amalek came and waged war against Israel. [9] Moses, therefore, said to Joshua, "Pick out certain men, and tomorrow go out and engage Amalek in battle. I will be standing on top of the hill with the staff of God in my hand." [10]So Joshua did as Moses told him: he engaged Amalek in battle after Moses had climbed to the top of the hill with Aaron and Hur. [11]As long as Moses kept his hands raised up, Israel had the better of the fight, but when he let his hands rest, Amalek had the better of the fight. [12]Moses' hands, however, grew tired; so they put a rock in place for him to sit on. Meanwhile Aaron and Hur supported his hands, one on one side and one on the other, so that his hands remained steady till sunset. [13]And Joshua mowed down Amalek and his people with the edge of the sword.

Responsorial Psalm: Psalms 121:1-2, 3-4, 5-6, 7-8

R. (cf. 2) **Our help is from the Lord, who made**
     heaven and earth.

[1] I lift up my eyes toward the mountains;
     whence shall help come to me?
[2] My help is from the LORD,
     who made heaven and earth.

R. **Our help is from the Lord, who made heaven**
     and earth.

[3] May he not suffer your foot to slip;
     may he slumber not who guards you:
[4] indeed he neither slumbers nor sleeps,
     the guardian of Israel.

R. **Our help is from the Lord, who made heaven**
     and earth.

[5] The LORD is your guardian; the LORD is your
          shade;
     he is beside you at your right hand.
[6] The sun shall not harm you by day,

nor the moon by night.

R. Our help is from the Lord, who made heaven and earth.

[7] The LORD will guard you from all evil;
he will guard your life.

[8] The LORD will guard your coming and your going,
both now and forever.

R. Our help is from the Lord, who made heaven and earth.

Second Reading: 2 Timothy 3:14-4:2

Beloved: [14]Remain faithful to what you have learned and believed, because you know from whom you learned it, [15]and that from infancy you have known the sacred Scriptures, which are capable of giving you wisdom for salvation through faith in Christ Jesus. [16]All Scripture is inspired by God and is useful for teaching, for refutation, for correction, and for training in righteousness, [17]so that one who belongs to God may be competent, equipped for every good work.

[1]I charge you in the presence of God and of Christ Jesus, who will judge the living and the dead, and by his appearing and his kingly power: [2]proclaim the word; be persistent whether it is convenient or inconvenient; convince, reprimand, encourage through all patience and teaching.

Alleluia: Hebrews 4:12

R. Alleluia, alleluia.

[12]The word of God is living and effective,
discerning reflections and thoughts of the heart.

R. Alleluia, alleluia.

Gospel: Luke 18:1-8

[1]Jesus told his disciples a parable about the necessity for them to pray always without becoming weary. [2] He said, "There was a judge in a certain town who neither feared God nor respected any human being. [3]And a widow in that town used to come to him and say, 'Render a just decision for me against my adversary.' [4]For a long time, the judge was unwilling, but eventually, he thought, 'While it is true that I neither fear God nor respect any human being, [5]because this widow keeps bothering me I shall deliver a just decision for her lest she finally come and strike me.'" [6]The Lord said, "Pay attention to what the dishonest judge says. [7]Will not God then secure the rights of his chosen ones who call out to him day and night? Will he be slow to answer them? [8]I tell you, he will see to it that justice is done for them speedily. But when the Son of Man comes, will he find faith on earth?"

Sunday October 26, 2025
Thirtieth Sunday in Ordinary Time, Year C

First Reading: Sirach 35:15BC-17, 20-22AB

15BCThe LORD is a God of justice,
who knows no favorites.
16Though not unduly partial toward the weak,
yet he hears the cry of the oppressed.
17The Lord is not deaf to the wail of the
orphan,
nor to the widow when she pours out her
complaint.
20The one who serves God willingly is heard;
his petition reaches the heavens.
21The prayer of the lowly pierces the clouds;
it does not rest till it reaches its goal,
nor will it withdraw till the Most High
responds,
22ABjudges justly and affirms the right,
and the Lord will not delay.

Responsorial Psalm: Psalms 34:2-3, 17-18, 19, 23

R. (7a) *The Lord hears the cry of the poor.*
2 I will bless the LORD at all times;
his praise shall be ever in my mouth.
3 Let my soul glory in the LORD;
the lowly will hear me and be glad.
R. *The Lord hears the cry of the poor.*
17 The LORD confronts the evildoers,
to destroy remembrance of them from
the earth.
18 When the just cry out, the LORD hears them,
and from all their distress he rescues
them.
R. *The Lord hears the cry of the poor.*
19The LORD is close to the brokenhearted;
and those who are crushed in spirit he
saves.
23The LORD redeems the lives of his servants;
no one incurs guilt who takes refuge in
him.
R. *The Lord hears the cry of the poor.*

Second Reading: 2 Timothy 4:6-8, 16-18

Beloved: 6I am already being poured out like a libation, and the time of my departure is at hand. 7I have competed well; I have finished the race; I have kept the faith. 8From now on the crown of righteousness awaits me, which the Lord, the just judge, will award to me on that day, and not only to me, but to all who have longed for his appearance.

[16]At my first defense no one appeared on my behalf, but everyone deserted me. May it not be held against them! [17]But the Lord stood by me and gave me strength, so that through me the proclamation might be completed and all the Gentiles might hear it. And I was rescued from the lion's mouth. [8]The Lord will rescue me from every evil threat and will bring me safe to his heavenly kingdom. To him be glory forever and ever. Amen.

Alleluia: 2 Corinthians 5:19
R. Alleluia, alleluia.
[19]God was reconciling the world to himself in
     Christ,
and entrusting to us the message of
     salvation.
R. Alleluia, alleluia.

Gospel: Luke 18:9-14
[9]Jesus addressed this parable to those who were convinced of their own righteousness and despised everyone else. [10]"Two people went up to the temple area to pray; one was a Pharisee and the other was a tax collector. [11]The Pharisee took up his position and spoke this prayer to himself, 'O God, I thank you that I am not like the rest of humanity— greedy, dishonest, adulterous— or even like this tax collector. [12]I fast twice a week, and I pay tithes on my whole income.' [13]But the tax collector stood off at a distance and would not even raise his eyes to heaven but beat his breast and prayed, 'O God, be merciful to me a sinner.' [14]I tell you, the latter went home justified, not the former; for whoever exalts himself will be humbled, and the one who humbles himself will be exalted."

NOVEMBER 2025
Sunday November 2, 2025

Commemoration of All the Faithful Departed – All Souls Day
(The following are a selection of the readings that may be chosen for this day. Other alternative readings are: Wisdom 4:7-15, Psalm 25, Philippians 3:20-21, and John 11:25a, 26 or Isaiah 25:6-9, Psalm 27:1, 4, 7, 8b, 13-14, 2 Corinthians 4:14-5:1, and John 14:1-6)

First Reading: Wisdom 3:1-9
[1] The souls of the just are in the hand of
     God,
    and no torment shall touch them.
[2] They seemed, in the view of the foolish,
      to be dead;
    and their passing away was thought
      an affliction

³ and their going forth from us, utter
      destruction.
But they are in peace.
⁴ For if before men, indeed, they be
         punished,
      yet is their hope full of immortality;
⁵ chastised a little, they shall be greatly
         blessed,
      because God tried them
      and found them worthy of himself.
⁶ As gold in the furnace, he proved them,
      and as sacrificial offerings he took
         them to himself.
⁷ In the time of their visitation they shall
         shine,
      and shall dart about as sparks
         through stubble;
⁸ they shall judge nations and rule over
         peoples,
      and the LORD shall be their King
         forever.
⁹ Those who trust in him shall understand
         truth,
      and the faithful shall abide with him
         in love:
because grace and mercy are with his
         holy ones,
      and his care is with his elect.

Responsorial Psalm: Psalms 23:1-3A, 3B-4, 5, 6
R. *(1)* **The Lord is my shepherd; there is nothing
         I shall want.**

or:

**Though I walk in the valley of darkness, I
         fear no evil, for you are with me.**
¹ The LORD is my shepherd; I shall not
         want.
      ² In verdant pastures he gives me
         repose;
beside restful waters he leads me;
      ^{3A} he refreshes my soul.
**R. The Lord is my shepherd; there is nothing
         I shall want.**

or:

Though I walk in the valley of darkness, I

fear no evil, for you are with me.
^{3B} He guides me in right paths
    for his name's sake.
⁴ Even though I walk in the dark valley
    I fear no evil; for you are at my side
with your rod and your staff
    that give me courage.
R. The Lord is my shepherd; there is nothing
    I shall want.

or:
Though I walk in the valley of darkness, I
    fear no evil, for you are with me.
⁵ You spread the table before me
    in the sight of my foes;
You anoint my head with oil;
    my cup overflows.
R. The Lord is my shepherd; there is nothing
    I shall want.

or:
Though I walk in the valley of darkness, I
    fear no evil, for you are with me.
⁶ Only goodness and kindness follow me
    all the days of my life;
and I shall dwell in the house of the LORD
    for years to come.
R. The Lord is my shepherd; there is nothing
    I shall want.

or:
Though I walk in the valley of darkness, I
    fear no evil, for you are with me.

Second Reading: Romans 5:5-11

Brothers and sisters: ⁵ Hope does not disappoint, because the love of God has been poured out into our hearts through the Holy Spirit that has been given to us. ⁶ For Christ, while we were still helpless, died at the appointed time for the ungodly. ⁷ Indeed, only with difficulty does one die for a just person, though perhaps for a good person one might even find courage to die. ⁸ But God proves his love for us in that while we were still sinners Christ died for us. ⁹ How much more then, since we are now justified by his Blood, will we be saved through him from the wrath. ¹⁰ Indeed, if, while we were enemies, we were reconciled to God through the death of his Son, how much more, once reconciled, will we be saved by his life. ¹¹ Not only that, but we also boast of God through our Lord Jesus Christ, through whom we have now received reconciliation.

Or Romans 6:3-9

Brothers and sisters: ³ Are you unaware that we who were baptized into Christ Jesus were baptized into his death? ⁴ We were indeed buried with him through baptism into death, so that, just as Christ was raised from the dead by the glory of the Father, we too might live in newness of life.

⁵ For if we have grown into union with him through a death like his, we shall also be united with him in the resurrection. ⁶ We know that our old self was crucified with him, so that our sinful body might be done away with, that we might no longer be in slavery to sin. ⁷ For a dead person has been absolved from sin. ⁸ If, then, we have died with Christ, we believe that we shall also live with him. ⁹ We know that Christ, raised from the dead, dies no more; death no longer has power over him.

Alleluia: Matthew 25:34
R. Alleluia, alleluia.
³⁴ Come, you who are blessed by
        my Father;
inherit the kingdom prepared
for you from the foundation of
        the world.
R. Alleluia, alleluia.

Gospel: John 6:37-40
Jesus said to the crowds: ³⁷ "Everything that the Father gives me will come to me, and I will not reject anyone who comes to me, ³⁸ because I came down from heaven not to do my own will but the will of the one who sent me. ³⁹ And this is the will of the one who sent me, that I should not lose anything of what he gave me, but that I should raise it on the last day. ⁴⁰ For this is the will of my Father, that everyone who sees the Son and believes in him may have eternal life, and I shall raise him on the last day."

Sunday November 9, 2025
Feast of Dedication of the Lateran Basilica in Rome
First Reading: Ezekiel 47:1-2, 8-9, 12
¹ The angel brought me back to the entrance of the temple, and I saw water flowing out from beneath the threshold of the temple toward the east, for the façade of the temple was toward the east; the water flowed down from the southern side of the temple, south of the altar. ² He led me outside by the north gate, and around to the outer gate facing the east, where I saw water trickling from the southern side. ⁸ He said to me, "This water flows into the eastern district down upon the Arabah, and empties into the sea, the salt waters, which it makes fresh. ⁹ Wherever the river flows, every sort of living creature that can multiply shall live, and there shall be abundant fish, for wherever this water comes the sea shall be made fresh. ¹² Along both banks of the river, fruit trees of every kind shall grow; their leaves shall not fade, nor their fruit fail. Every month they shall bear fresh fruit, for they shall be watered by the flow from the sanctuary. Their fruit shall serve for food, and their leaves for medicine."

Responsorial Psalm: Psalms 46:2-3, 5-6, 8-9

R. (5) The waters of the river gladden the city of God, the holy dwelling of the Most High!

2 God is our refuge and our strength,
   an ever-present help in distress.
3 Therefore, we fear not, though the earth be shaken
   and mountains plunge into the depths of the sea.

R. The waters of the river gladden the city of God, the holy dwelling of the Most High!

5 There is a stream whose runlets gladden the city of God,
   the holy dwelling of the Most High.
6 God is in its midst; it shall not be disturbed;
   God will help it at the break of dawn.

R. The waters of the river gladden the city of God, the holy dwelling of the Most High!

8 The LORD of hosts is with us;
   our stronghold is the God of Jacob.
9 Come! behold the deeds of the LORD,
   the astounding things he has wrought on earth.

R. The waters of the river gladden the city of God, the holy dwelling of the Most High!

Second Reading: 1 Corinthians 3:9C-11, 16-17

Brothers and sisters: 9C You are God's building. 10 According to the grace of God given to me, like a wise master builder I laid a foundation, and another is building upon it. But each one must be careful how he builds upon it, 11 for no one can lay a foundation other than the one that is there, namely, Jesus Christ.

16 Do you not know that you are the temple of God, and that the Spirit of God dwells in you? 17 If anyone destroys God's temple, God will destroy that person; for the temple of God, which you are, is holy.

Alleluia: 2 Chronicles 7:16

R. Alleluia, alleluia.

16 I have chosen and consecrated this house,
   says the Lord,

that my name may be there forever.
R. Alleluia, alleluia.

Gospel: John 2:13-22

[13] Since the Passover of the Jews was near, Jesus went up to Jerusalem. [14] He found in the temple area those who sold oxen, sheep, and doves, as well as the money-changers seated there. [15] He made a whip out of cords and drove them all out of the temple area, with the sheep and oxen, and spilled the coins of the money-changers and overturned their tables, [16] and to those who sold doves he said, "Take these out of here, and stop making my Father's house a marketplace." [17] His disciples recalled the words of Scripture, *Zeal for your house will consume me*. [18] At this the Jews answered and said to him, "What sign can you show us for doing this?" [19] Jesus answered and said to them, "Destroy this temple and in three days I will raise it up." [20] The Jews said, "This temple has been under construction for forty-six years, and you will raise it up in three days?" [21] But he was speaking about the temple of his Body. [22] Therefore, when he was raised from the dead, his disciples remembered that he had said this, and they came to believe the Scripture and the word Jesus had spoken.

Sunday November 16, 2025

Thirty-third Sunday in Ordinary Time, Year C

First Reading: Malachi 3:19-20A

[19] Lo, the day is coming, blazing like an oven,
when all the proud and all evildoers will
be stubble,
and the day that is coming will set them on
fire,
leaving them neither root nor branch,
says the LORD of hosts.
[20A]But for you who fear my name, there will
arise
the sun of justice with its healing rays.

Responsorial Psalm: Psalms 98:5-6, 7-8, 9

R. [cf. 9] **The Lord comes to rule the earth with justice.**
[5] Sing praise to the LORD with the harp,
with the harp and melodious song.
[6] With trumpets and the sound of the horn
sing joyfully before the King, the LORD.
R. The Lord comes to rule the earth with justice.
[7] Let the sea and what fills it resound,
the world and those who dwell in it;
[8] let the rivers clap their hands,
the mountains shout with them for joy.

R. The Lord comes to rule the earth with justice.
[9] Before the LORD, for he comes,
    for he comes to rule the earth;
he will rule the world with justice
    and the peoples with equity.
R. The Lord comes to rule the earth with justice.

Second Reading: 2 Thessalonians 3:7-12

Brothers and sisters: [7]You know how one must imitate us. For we did not act in a disorderly way among you, [8]nor did we eat food received free from anyone. On the contrary, in toil and drudgery, night and day we worked, so as not to burden any of you. [9]Not that we do not have the right. Rather, we wanted to present ourselves as a model for you, so that you might imitate us. [10]In fact, when we were with you, we instructed you that if anyone was unwilling to work, neither should that one eat. [11]We hear that some are conducting themselves among you in a disorderly way, by not keeping busy but minding the business of others. [12]Such people we instruct and urge in the Lord Jesus Christ to work quietly and to eat their own food.

Alleluia: Luke 21:28

R. Alleluia, alleluia.
[28] Stand erect and raise your heads
because your redemption is at hand.
R. Alleluia, alleluia.

Gospel: Luke 21:5-19

[5]While some people were speaking about how the temple was adorned with costly stones and votive offerings, Jesus said, [6]"All that you see here— the days will come when there will not be left a stone upon another stone that will not be thrown down."

[7]Then they asked him, "Teacher, when will this happen? And what sign will there be when all these things are about to happen?" [8]He answered, "See that you not be deceived, for many will come in my name, saying, 'I am he,' and 'The time has come.' Do not follow them! [9]When you hear of wars and insurrections, do not be terrified; for such things must happen first, but it will not immediately be the end." [10]Then he said to them, "Nation will rise against nation, and kingdom against kingdom. [11]There will be powerful earthquakes, famines, and plagues from place to place; and awesome sights and mighty signs will come from the sky.

[12]"Before all this happens, however, they will seize and persecute you, they will hand you over to the synagogues and to prisons, and they will have you led before kings and governors because of my name. [13]It will lead to your giving testimony. [14]Remember, you are not to prepare your defense beforehand, [15]for I myself shall give you a wisdom in speaking that all your adversaries will be powerless to resist or refute. [16]You will even be handed over by parents, brothers, relatives, and friends, and they will put some of you to death. [17]You will be hated by all because of my name, [18]but not

a hair on your head will be destroyed. [19]By your perseverance you will secure your lives."

Feast of Christ the Universal King, Year C
First Reading: 2 Samuel 5:1-3

[1]In those days, all the tribes of Israel came to David in Hebron and said: "Here we are, your bone and your flesh. [2]In days past, when Saul was our king, it was you who led the Israelites out and brought them back. And the LORD said to you, 'You shall shepherd my people Israel and shall be commander of Israel.'" [3]When all the elders of Israel came to David in Hebron, King David made an agreement with them there before the LORD, and they anointed him king of Israel.

Responsorial Psalm: Psalms 122:1-2, 3-4, 4-5

R. [(cf. 1)] **Let us go rejoicing to the house of the Lord.**

[1]I rejoiced because they said to me,
    "We will go up to the house of the LORD."
[2] And now we have set foot
    within your gates, O Jerusalem.
R. **Let us go rejoicing to the house of the Lord.**

[3]Jerusalem, built as a city
    with compact unity.
[4AB]To it the tribes go up,
    the tribes of the LORD.
R. **Let us go rejoicing to the house of the Lord.**

[4CD]According to the decree for Israel,
    to give thanks to the name of the LORD.
[5]In it are set up judgment seats,
    seats for the house of David.
R. **Let us go rejoicing to the house of the Lord.**

Second Reading: Colossians 1:12-20

Brothers and sisters: [12]Let us give thanks to the Father, who has made you fit to share in the inheritance of the holy ones in light. [13]He delivered us from the power of darkness and transferred us to the kingdom of his beloved Son, [14]in whom we have redemption, the forgiveness of sins.

[15]He is the image of the invisible God,
    the firstborn of all creation.
[16]For in him were created all things in heaven
        and on earth,
    the visible and the invisible,
    whether thrones or dominions or
        principalities or powers;
    all things were created through him and

for him.
^{17}He is before all things,
	and in him all things hold together.
^{18}He is the head of the body, the church.
He is the beginning, the firstborn from the
		dead,
	that in all things he himself might be
		preeminent.
^{19}For in him all the fullness was pleased to
		dwell,
	^{20}and through him to reconcile all things
		for him,
	making peace by the blood of his cross
	through him, whether those on earth or
		those in heaven.

Alleluia: Mark 11:9, 10
R. Alleluia, alleluia.
^{9} Blessed is he who comes in the name of the
		Lord!
^{10} Blessed is the kingdom of our father David
		that is to come!
R. Alleluia, alleluia.

Gospel: Luke 23:35-43
^{35}The rulers sneered at Jesus and said, "He saved others, let him save himself if he is the chosen one, the Christ of God." ^{36}Even the soldiers jeered at him. As they approached to offer him wine ^{37}they called out, "If you are King of the Jews, save yourself." ^{38}Above him there was an inscription that read, "This is the King of the Jews."

^{39}Now one of the criminals hanging there reviled Jesus, saying, "Are you not the Christ? Save yourself and us." ^{40}The other, however, rebuking him, said in reply, "Have you no fear of God, for you are subject to the same condemnation? ^{41}And indeed, we have been condemned justly, for the sentence we received corresponds to our crimes, but this man has done nothing criminal." ^{42}Then he said, "Jesus, remember me when you come into your kingdom." ^{43}He replied to him, "Amen, I say to you, today you will be with me in Paradise."

Sunday November 30, 2025
First Sunday of Advent, Year A
First Reading: Isaiah 2:1-5
^{1}This is what Isaiah, son of Amoz, saw concerning Judah and Jerusalem.

^{2}In days to come,
the mountain of the LORD's house
	shall be established as the highest

mountain
and raised above the hills.
All nations shall stream toward it;
[3]many peoples shall come and say:
"Come, let us climb the LORD's mountain,
to the house of the God of Jacob,
that he may instruct us in his ways,
and we may walk in his paths."
For from Zion shall go forth instruction,
and the word of the LORD from Jerusalem.
[4]He shall judge between the nations,
and impose terms on many peoples.
They shall beat their swords into plowshares
and their spears into pruning hooks;
one nation shall not raise the sword against
another,
nor shall they train for war again.
[5]O house of Jacob, come,
let us walk in the light of the LORD!

Responsorial Psalm: Psalms 122: 1-2, 3-4, 4-5, 6-7, 8-9
R. Let us go rejoicing to the house of the Lord.
[1] I rejoiced because they said to me,
"We will go up to the house of the LORD."
[2] And now we have set foot
within your gates, O Jerusalem.
R. Let us go rejoicing to the house of the Lord.
[3] Jerusalem, built as a city
with compact unity.
[4] To it the tribes go up,
the tribes of the LORD.
R. Let us go rejoicing to the house of the Lord.
[4] According to the decree for Israel,
to give thanks to the name of the LORD.
[5] In it are set up judgment seats,
seats for the house of David.
R. Let us go rejoicing to the house of the Lord.
[6] Pray for the peace of Jerusalem!
May those who love you prosper!
[7] May peace be within your walls,
prosperity in your buildings.
R. Let us go rejoicing to the house of the Lord.
[8] Because of my brothers and friends
I will say, "Peace be within you!"
[9] Because of the house of the LORD, our God,

I will pray for your good.
R. Let us go rejoicing to the house of the Lord.

Second Reading: Romans 13:11-14

Brothers and sisters: [11]You know the time; it is the hour now for you to awake from sleep. For our salvation is nearer now than when we first believed; [12]the night is advanced, the day is at hand. Let us then throw off the works of darkness and put on the armor of light; [13]let us conduct ourselves properly as in the day, not in orgies and drunkenness, not in promiscuity and lust, not in rivalry and jealousy. [14]But put on the Lord Jesus Christ, and make no provision for the desires of the flesh.

Alleluia: cf. Psalms 85:8

R. Alleluia, alleluia.
[8] Show us, Lord, your love;
and grant us your salvation.
R. Alleluia, alleluia.

Gospel: Matthew 24:37-44

[37]Jesus said to his disciples: "As it was in the days of Noah, so it will be at the coming of the Son of Man. [38]In those days before the flood, they were eating and drinking, marrying and giving in marriage, up to the day that Noah entered the ark. [39]They did not know until the flood came and carried them all away. So will it be also at the coming of the Son of Man. [40]Two men will be out in the field; one will be taken, and one will be left. [41]Two women will be grinding at the mill; one will be taken, and one will be left. [42]Therefore, stay awake! For you do not know on which day your Lord will come. [43]Be sure of this: if the master of the house had known the hour of night when the thief was coming, he would have stayed awake and not let his house be broken into. [44]So too, you also must be prepared, for at an hour you do not expect, the Son of Man will come."

DECEMBER 2025
Sunday December 7, 2025
Second Sunday of Advent, Year A

First Reading: Isaiah 11:1-10

[1]On that day, a shoot shall sprout from the
	stump of Jesse,
	and from his roots a bud shall blossom.
[2]The spirit of the LORD shall rest upon him:

a spirit of wisdom and of understanding,
a spirit of counsel and of strength,
a spirit of knowledge and of fear of the
LORD,
³and his delight shall be the fear of the
LORD.
Not by appearance shall he judge,
nor by hearsay shall he decide,
⁴but he shall judge the poor with justice,
and decide aright for the land's afflicted.
He shall strike the ruthless with the rod of
his mouth,
and with the breath of his lips he shall
slay the wicked.
⁵Justice shall be the band around his waist,
and faithfulness a belt upon his hips.
⁶Then the wolf shall be a guest of the
lamb,
and the leopard shall lie down with the
kid;
the calf and the young lion shall browse
together,
with a little child to guide them.
⁷The cow and the bear shall be neighbors,
together their young shall rest;
the lion shall eat hay like the ox.
⁸The baby shall play by the cobra's den,
and the child lay his hand on the adder's
lair.
⁹There shall be no harm or ruin on all my
holy mountain;
for the earth shall be filled with
knowledge of the LORD,
as water covers the sea.
¹⁰On that day, the root of Jesse,
set up as a signal for the nations,
the Gentiles shall seek out,
for his dwelling shall be glorious.

Responsorial Psalm: Psalms 72:1-2, 7-8, 12-13, 17

R. (cf. 7) *Justice shall flourish in his time, and*
fullness of peace for ever.
¹O God, with your judgment endow the king,
and with your justice, the king's son;
² he shall govern your people with justice

and your afflicted ones with judgment.

R. Justice shall flourish in his time, and fullness of peace for ever.

⁷Justice shall flower in his days,
 and profound peace, till the moon be no
  more.
⁸May he rule from sea to sea,
 and from the River to the ends of the
  earth.

R. Justice shall flourish in his time, and fullness of peace for ever.

¹²For he shall rescue the poor when he cries
  out,
 and the afflicted when he has no one to
  help him.
¹³He shall have pity for the lowly and the
  poor;
 the lives of the poor he shall save.

R. Justice shall flourish in his time, and fullness of peace for ever.

¹⁷May his name be blessed forever;
 as long as the sun his name shall remain.
In him shall all the tribes of the earth be
  blessed;
 all the nations shall proclaim his
  happiness.

R. Justice shall flourish in his time, and fullness of peace for ever.

Second Reading: Romans 15:4-9

Brothers and sisters: ⁴Whatever was written previously was written for our instruction, that by endurance and by the encouragement of the Scriptures we might have hope. ⁵May the God of endurance and encouragement grant you to think in harmony with one another, in keeping with Christ Jesus, ⁶that with one accord you may with one voice glorify the God and Father of our Lord Jesus Christ.

⁷Welcome one another, then, as Christ welcomed you, for the glory of God. ⁸For I say that Christ became a minister of the circumcised to show God's truthfulness, to confirm the promises to the patriarchs, ⁹but so that the Gentiles might glorify God for his mercy. As it is written:

Therefore, I will praise you among the
 Gentiles
 and sing praises to your name.

Alleluia: Luke 3:4, 6

R. Alleluia, alleluia.

⁴Prepare the way of the Lord, make straight
     his paths:
⁶all flesh shall see the salvation of God.

R. Alleluia, alleluia.

Gospel: Matthew 3:1-12

¹John the Baptist appeared, preaching in the desert of Judea ²and saying, "Repent, for the kingdom of heaven is at hand!" ³It was of him that the prophet Isaiah had spoken when he said:

A voice of one crying out in the desert,
Prepare the way of the Lord,
    make straight his paths.

⁴John wore clothing made of camel's hair and had a leather belt around his waist. His food was locusts and wild honey. ⁵At that time Jerusalem, all Judea, and the whole region around the Jordan were going out to him ⁶and were being baptized by him in the Jordan River as they acknowledged their sins. ⁷When he saw many of the Pharisees and Sadducees coming to his baptism, he said to them, "You brood of vipers! Who warned you to flee from the coming wrath? ⁸Produce good fruit as evidence of your repentance. ⁹And do not presume to say to yourselves, 'We have Abraham as our father.' For I tell you, God can raise up children to Abraham from these stones. ¹⁰Even now the ax lies at the root of the trees. Therefore every tree that does not bear good fruit will be cut down and thrown into the fire. ¹¹I am baptizing you with water, for repentance, but the one who is coming after me is mightier than I. I am not worthy to carry his sandals. He will baptize you with the Holy Spirit and fire. ¹²His winnowing fan is in his hand. He will clear his threshing floor and gather his wheat into his barn, but the chaff he will burn with unquenchable fire."

Sunday December 14, 2025
Third Sunday of Advent, Year A

First Reading: Isaiah 35:1-6A, 10

¹The desert and the parched land will exult;
    the steppe will rejoice and bloom.
² They will bloom with abundant flowers,
    and rejoice with joyful song.
The glory of Lebanon will be given to them,
    the splendor of Carmel and Sharon;
they will see the glory of the LORD,
    the splendor of our God.
    ³Strengthen the hands that are feeble,
    make firm the knees that are weak,

⁴say to those whose hearts are frightened:
    Be strong, fear not!
Here is your God,
    he comes with vindication;
with divine recompense
    he comes to save you.
⁵Then will the eyes of the blind be opened,
    the ears of the deaf be cleared;
⁶then will the lame leap like a stag,
    then the tongue of the mute will sing.

¹⁰Those whom the LORD has ransomed will
        return
    and enter Zion singing,
    crowned with everlasting joy;
they will meet with joy and gladness,
    sorrow and mourning will flee.

Responsorial Psalm: Psalms 146:6-7,8-9,9-10

R. *(cf. Is 35:4)* **Lord, come and save us.** or: *R. Alleluia.*
⁶The LORD God keeps faith forever,
    ⁷secures justice for the oppressed,
    gives food to the hungry.
The LORD sets captives free.
R. Lord, come and save us. or: *R. Alleluia.*
⁸The LORD gives sight to the blind;
    the LORD raises up those who were bowed
        down.
The LORD loves the just;
    ⁹ᴬthe LORD protects strangers.
R. Lord, come and save us. or: *R. Alleluia.*
⁹ᴮᶜThe fatherless and the widow he sustains,
    but the way of the wicked he thwarts.
¹⁰The LORD shall reign forever;
    your God, O Zion, through all
        generations.
R. Lord, come and save us. or: *R. Alleluia.*

Second Reading: James 5:7-10

⁷Be patient, brothers and sisters, until the coming of the Lord. See how the farmer waits for the precious fruit of the earth, being patient with it until it receives the early and the late rains. ⁸You too must be patient. Make your hearts firm, because the coming of the Lord is at hand. ⁹Do not complain, brothers and sisters, about one another, that you may not be judged. Behold, the Judge is standing before the gates.

[10]Take as an example of hardship and patience, brothers and sisters, the prophets who spoke in the name of the Lord.

Alleluia: Isaiah 61:1 (cited in Luke 4:18)
R. Alleluia, alleluia.
[18]The Spirit of the Lord is upon me,
because he has anointed me
to bring glad tidings to the poor.
R. Alleluia, alleluia.

Gospel: Matthew 11:2-11
[2]When John the Baptist heard in prison of the works of the Christ, he sent his disciples to Jesus [3]with this question, "Are you the one who is to come, or should we look for another?" [4]Jesus said to them in reply, "Go and tell John what you hear and see: [5]the blind regain their sight, the lame walk, lepers are cleansed, the deaf hear, the dead are raised, and the poor have the good news proclaimed to them. [6]And blessed is the one who takes no offense at me."

[7]As they were going off, Jesus began to speak to the crowds about John, "What did you go out to the desert to see? A reed swayed by the wind? [8]Then what did you go out to see? Someone dressed in fine clothing? Those who wear fine clothing are in royal palaces. [9]Then why did you go out? To see a prophet? Yes, I tell you, and more than a prophet. [10]This is the one about whom it is written:

Behold, I am sending my messenger ahead of
*   you;*
he will prepare your way before you.

[11]Amen, I say to you, among those born of women there has been none greater than John the Baptist; yet the least in the kingdom of heaven is greater than he."

Sunday December 21, 2025
Fourth Sunday of Advent, Year A
First Reading: Isaiah 7:10-14
[10]The LORD spoke to Ahaz, saying: [11]Ask for a sign from the LORD, your God; let it be deep as the netherworld, or high as the sky! [12]But Ahaz answered, "I will not ask! I will not tempt the LORD!" [13]Then Isaiah said: Listen, O house of David! Is it not enough for you to weary people, must you also weary my God? [14]Therefore the Lord himself will give you this sign: the virgin shall conceive, and bear a son, and shall name him Emmanuel.

Responsorial Psalm: Psalms 24:1-2, 3-4, 5-6
R. *(7c and 10b)* **Let the Lord enter; he is king of glory.**
[1]The LORD's are the earth and its fullness;
        the world and those who dwell in it.

²For he founded it upon the seas
   and established it upon the rivers.
R. Let the Lord enter; he is king of glory.
³Who can ascend the mountain of the LORD?
   or who may stand in his holy place?
⁴One whose hands are sinless, whose heart is
      clean,
   who desires not what is vain.
R. Let the Lord enter; he is king of glory.
⁵He shall receive a blessing from the LORD,
   a reward from God his savior.
⁶Such is the race that seeks for him,
   that seeks the face of the God of Jacob.
R. Let the Lord enter; he is king of glory.

Second Reading: Romans 1:1-7
¹Paul, a slave of Christ Jesus, called to be an apostle and set apart for the gospel of God, ²which he promised previously through his prophets in the holy Scriptures, ³the gospel about his Son, descended from David according to the flesh, ⁴but established as Son of God in power according to the Spirit of holiness through resurrection from the dead, Jesus Christ our Lord. ⁵Through him we have received the grace of apostleship, to bring about the obedience of faith, for the sake of his name, among all the Gentiles, ⁶among whom are you also, who are called to belong to Jesus Christ; ⁷to all the beloved of God in Rome, called to be holy. Grace to you and peace from God our Father and the Lord Jesus Christ.

Alleluia: Matthew 1:23
R. Alleluia, alleluia.
²³The virgin shall conceive, and bear a son,
and they shall name him Emmanuel.
R. Alleluia, alleluia.

Gospel: Matthew 1:18-24
¹⁸This is how the birth of Jesus Christ came about. When his mother Mary was betrothed to Joseph, but before they lived together, she was found with child through the Holy Spirit. ¹⁹Joseph her husband, since he was a righteous man, yet unwilling to expose her to shame, decided to divorce her quietly. ²⁰Such was his intention when, behold, the angel of the Lord appeared to him in a dream and said, "Joseph, son of David, do not be afraid to take Mary your wife into your home. For it is through the Holy Spirit that this child has been conceived in her. ²¹She will bear a son and you are to name him Jesus, because he will save his people from their sins." ²²All this took place to fulfill what the Lord had said through the prophet:

²³*Behold, the virgin shall conceive and bear a*

son,
    and they shall name him Emmanuel,

which means "God is with us." ²⁴When Joseph awoke, he did as the angel of the Lord had commanded him and took his wife into his home.

Sunday December 28, 2025
Feast of the Holy Family of Jesus, Mary and Joseph
First Reading: Sirach 3:2-6, 12-14

² God sets a father in honor over his
        children;
    a mother's authority he confirms
        over her sons.
³ Whoever honors his father atones for
        sins,
    and preserves himself from them.
When he prays, he is heard;
      ⁴ he stores up riches who reveres his
        mother.
⁵ Whoever honors his father is gladdened
        by children,
    and, when he prays, is heard.
⁶ Whoever reveres his father will live a
        long life;
    he who obeys his father brings
        comfort to his mother.

¹² My son, take care of your father when
        he is old;
    grieve him not as long as he lives.
¹³ Even if his mind fail, be considerate of
        him;
    revile him not all the days of his life;
¹⁴ kindness to a father will not be
        forgotten,
    firmly planted against the debt of
        your sins
—a house raised in justice to you.

Responsorial Psalm: Psalms 128:1-2, 3, 4-5.
R. *(cf. 1)* **Blessed are those who fear the Lord and
        walk in his ways.**
¹ Blessed is everyone who fears the LORD,
    who walks in his ways!
² For you shall eat the fruit of your handiwork;

blessed shall you be, and favored.
R. Blessed are those who fear the Lord and walk
in his ways.
[3] Your wife shall be like a fruitful vine
in the recesses of your home;
your children like olive plants
around your table.
R. Blessed are those who fear the Lord and walk
in his ways.
[4] Behold, thus is the man blessed
who fears the LORD.
[5] The LORD bless you from Zion:
may you see the prosperity of Jerusalem
all the days of your life.
R. Blessed are those who fear the Lord and walk
in his ways.

Second Reading: Colossians 3:12-21

Brothers and sisters: [12] Put on, as God's chosen ones, holy and beloved, heartfelt compassion, kindness, humility, gentleness, and patience, [13] bearing with one another and forgiving one another, if one has a grievance against another; as the Lord has forgiven you, so must you also do. [14] And over all these put on love, that is, the bond of perfection. [15] And let the peace of Christ control your hearts, the peace into which you were also called in one body. And be thankful. [16] Let the word of Christ dwell in you richly, as in all wisdom you teach and admonish one another, singing psalms, hymns, and spiritual songs with gratitude in your hearts to God. [17] And whatever you do, in word or in deed, do everything in the name of the Lord Jesus, giving thanks to God the Father through him.

[18] Wives, be subordinate to your husbands, as is proper in the Lord. [19] Husbands, love your wives, and avoid any bitterness toward them. [20] Children, obey your parents in everything, for this is pleasing to the Lord. [21] Fathers, do not provoke your children, so they may not become discouraged.

Or Colossians 3:12-17

Brothers and sisters: [12] Put on, as God's chosen ones, holy and beloved, heartfelt compassion, kindness, humility, gentleness, and patience, [13] bearing with one another and forgiving one another, if one has a grievance against another; as the Lord has forgiven you, so must you also do. [14] And over all these put on love, that is, the bond of perfection. [15] And let the peace of Christ control your hearts, the peace into which you were also called in one body. And be thankful. [16] Let the word of Christ dwell in you richly, as in all wisdom you teach and admonish one another, singing psalms, hymns, and spiritual songs with gratitude in your hearts to God. [17] And whatever you do, in word or in deed, do everything in the name of the Lord Jesus, giving thanks to God the Father through him.

Alleluia: Colossians 3:15A, 16A
R. Alleluia, alleluia.
15A Let the peace of Christ control your hearts;
16A let the word of Christ dwell in you richly.
R. Alleluia, alleluia.

Gospel: Matthew 2:13-15; 19-23
13When the magi had departed, behold, the angel of the Lord appeared to Joseph in a dream and said, "Rise, take the child and his mother, flee to Egypt, and stay there until I tell you. Herod is going to search for the child to destroy him." 14 Joseph rose and took the child and his mother by night and departed for Egypt. 15 He stayed there until the death of Herod, that what the Lord had said through the prophet might be fulfilled, *Out of Egypt I called my son.*

19When Herod had died, behold, the angel of the Lord appeared in a dream to Joseph in Egypt 20 and said, "Rise, take the child and his mother and go to the land of Israel, for those who sought the child's life are dead." 21 He rose, took the child and his mother, and went to the land of Israel. 22 But when he heard that Archelaus was ruling over Judea in place of his father Herod, he was afraid to go back there. And because he had been warned in a dream, he departed for the region of Galilee. 23He went and dwelt in a town called Nazareth, so that what had been spoken through the prophets might be fulfilled, *He shall be called a Nazorean.*

For comments, suggestions, support, requests, and other pieces of information that might make our publication serve its audience better, kindly contact the director of Catholic Lectionary Publishers through email: okoraforinnocent977@gmail.com.

Printed in Great Britain
by Amazon

62384276R00078